RANDOM POSITIVE THOUGHTS

By

MINHAJ UDDIN

Absolute Author
Publishing House

Random Positive Thoughts
Minhaj Uddin
Copyright © 2020 by Minhaj Uddin
All Rights Reserved

Disclaimer

The information contained cannot be considered a substitute for treatment as prescribed by a therapist or other professional. By reading this book, you are assuming all risks associated with using the advice, data, and suggestions given below, with a full understanding that you, solely, are responsible for anything that may occur as a result of putting this information into action in any way – regardless of your interpretation of the advice.

Publisher: Absolute Author Publishing House
Editors: Emily Jones, Michele L Mathews, Alexa-Ray Coleman
Cover Designer: PixelStudio

LIBRARY OF CONGRESS CATALOGING IN-PUBLICATION-DATA

Uddin, Minhaj

Random Positive Thoughts/ Minhaj, Uddin

ISBN: 978-1-951028-88-6

1. Self-help

2. Motivational

3. Advice

CONTENTS

PREFACE

This book is a collection of positive thoughts and insights aimed at helping those who are feeling low, lack self-esteem, feel depressed, or have suicidal thoughts. Most people judge themselves based on the material things they possess and forget about their true value or inner worth as beings on this planet. We forget that life is short and that we will leave this world the way we came into it—without any material possessions. We get consumed with pleasuring our earthly bodies to the detriment of our souls. By worshipping the material things, we collect, we undoubtedly cause more harm to ourselves than good. This book makes useful insights through explaining and unpacking the true value of life through using examples, analogies, and true and fictional stories. These positive thoughts and insights will hopefully bring you the peace of mind that you have been searching for. Only a peaceful mind has the capacity and frequency needed to reconnect with higher intelligence. Only a focused mind attracts creativity and positivity and can make progress in life. Focusing on improving our inner lives rather than accumulating our external desires is vital to a peaceful existence. This can also help dissolve chronic stresses, which will positively influence our health and prevent diseases by boosting our immune system. We need our bodies to remain strong to achieve the success we desire. We have to start with our minds. Have you been craving for a calm and relaxed existence for a while now? If your answer is yes, this book is what you need.

I want to start by telling you about myself and how I came to embrace positivity in my life. I graduated in the field of nursing with a medical sciences degree and later, a postgraduate degree in health economics and management. During those years, I learnt about our global economies and how they relate to our health as beings: global markets, prices, products, their values, supply and demand. I also suffered from severe depression and suicidal thoughts at that time; it was such a dark time, and the pressure was too much. Slowly, I found myself in a space where I didn't want to do anything. I refused to meet my friends, my parents were angry at me, and even my weight fluctuated. To make things worse, I was in a dilemma about my career path. So, believe me when I tell you, I know how ugly and painful depression can be.

To get me out of this rut, I started reading spiritual books by Eckhart Tolle, Deepak Chopra, Don Miguel Ruiz, and others. Day by day, their words breathed life into me and allowed me to break the illusion and connect with reality. I began to break free from the chains of depression, and because of their words, I found ways to transmute my agony into joy. I had been working as a registered nurse for five years in the emergency room department in one of the best international humanitarian organizations, *Médecins Sans Frontières (MSF)*. I was used to dealing with different patients who suffered from depression, anxiety, panic attacks, and suicidal thoughts. I knew what the signs were. I had the privilege of working with young and old patients, getting to know them and treating them. Some were terminally ill and would share their life stories with me. I watched and observed and kept this knowledge until now. I have reached a point in my life where I can give back by sharing my life experiences and the knowledge I have gained. Combining my life experience, educational background, and the teachings from the books, I am here to share a message of positivity through valuable and positive insights. These insights helped not only me but also my colleagues, friends, and family members. Most of my friends and colleagues thank me for relieving them from the patterns of their negative thoughts.

As an emergency department nurse, I observed many patients who came to the emergency room with anxiety and depression and had attempted suicide. Some were saved, and some lost the battle for their lives. It pained me when the doctor declared the death of the suicidal patient to their relatives. This is the main reason that motivates me to write this book and share these positive thoughts. I hope to save others from low self-esteem, depression, and suicide by explaining to them that they have true value and infinite intelligence and potential. Many times, our egos can blind us from reality, and we start comparing ourselves to others. Material possessions can activate negative emotions and feelings, like jealousy, anxiety, and depression, which might lead the person to commit suicide in some extreme cases. Everyone has bad days and suffers from depression at some point in their lives, but the depression and bad days do not stay forever. They will dissipate sooner or later. I also had suicidal thoughts in my thirties, but I did not follow through. After a few months, my depression subsided, and until now, I have been living a good life, full of positive energy. I always remind myself that if I had committed suicide when I was depressed, I would have missed out on these fruitful and worthwhile experiences. I want to share with you that positive energy yields positive results. Yes, you can have low days, and you should embrace those feelings, then rise from them. We deserve your worth and presence in this world. Read on to find out about the secrets of leading a peaceful and positive existence.

ACKNOWLEDGMENT

First and foremost, I would like to express my utmost gratitude to Allah, the Creator of this universe, who gave me countless blessings, strength and courage to publish this book. Next, I am grateful and thankful to my parents – my mother and father. It is because of them, after Allah, that I have been able to write this book. It would not have been possible without their unwavering support and constant encouragement, and this book is dedicated to them.

I would like to acknowledge and thank all of my teachers who have inspired me in so many ways to pursue my passion. No doubt it is because of their hard work and guidance that I have been able to write this book. The process of writing is not an easy one. It takes a lot of focus and attention, requiring you to isolate yourself from everyone else and sit in front of screen thinking and typing. I am blessed that my siblings supported me wholeheartedly in my endeavors. They made sure that I was given the alone time, free of distractions, to focus on writing this book and making progress. I am grateful to them for all their help and support. Last, but not the least, I would like to express my heartfelt gratitude to my friends, who supported me in my hard time and encouraged me for writing this book.

INTRODUCTION

The purpose of this book is simple—to provide essential insights by sharing positive thoughts and critical information for those who are suffering from depression, anxiety, and low self-esteem. It caters to those who have suicidal thoughts because of real or perceived painful life situations. These insights will be developed through logical reasoning, examples, analogies, and short stories. Through combining all these aspects, we can sharpen our minds and increase our level of intelligence. This book covers a wide range of issues we need to understand: (1) the true value of life, (2) how valuable we are as humans, (3) the true value of materialistic things, (4) the importance of other people in our lives, (5) how we can achieve joy and happiness, (6) how intense pain can transform failure into success, (7) how we should cope with real or perceived painful life experiences, (8) how we can rise from failure to be successful, and much more. This book is an attempt to contribute to the improvement of the human condition and save us from negativity and, in some cases, death.

Humans are the most intelligent beings and have an extensive source of knowledge. Human minds have been evolving and learning things, drawing from life experiences and the knowledge shared by others. Numerous people share their teachings and life experiences with other people through mediums, such as books, podcasts, and webinars, and these people then learn a thing or two and share with others. It's a revolving door of sharing knowledge and understanding, spreading wisdom and guidance. Sometimes the knowledge is not useful, but many times it is. We have to figure out what works for us and what doesn't. This book is also a product of the human mind, intelligence, intuitions, and learning from experiences and other great people. To learn from others is the best way to see things from different angles. It's like switching on a light of wisdom, awareness, and consciousness, and thus, the spread of wisdom continues to save other people from darkness, insanity, and evil. After all, sharing is caring.

As I mentioned, this book is a collection of positive thoughts and insights, which I have learnt over my lifetime from other spiritual teachers and great people. My mind has been imbued with these positive thoughts and insights since my thirties when I was depressed because of multiple factors. Life wasn't going well for me, and I ended up in a dark and depressive space. One day, I was listening to the Linkin Park song called "In the End." The lyrics, "I tried so hard and got so far but in the end it doesn't even matter," prompted a reverie about the values and priorities I had adopted in my life. I started to think about the future and what would happen if I realized in my 60s or 70s that I had spent my whole life looking for things that had no value and wasted valuable years on meaningless bullshit. I was so fixated on external desires and issues. I blamed external things for my problems in life instead of looking within. Then I thought about the regret and despair I would feel having wasted years of vital growth. In that moment, I knew something had to change. I asked myself what I could do to turn things around and to make sure I didn't end up a grumpy old fart, complaining about everything and anything.

At that point, I had a bit of a revelation. I realized I had limited knowledge about things and actions and their values. I had been consumed about issues that were not important, which affected my decision-making process. I made poor decisions which led me to fail, accumulating regrets and despair. I eventually understood that I needed to add to my knowledge bank and learn to improve my decision-making processes to avoid being hopeless and regretful when I get older. So, I started to learn from other great people by reading and listening to their books and watching documentaries about them.

A wise man once said that "a smart man learns from his mistakes, a wise one learns from the mistakes of others," so learning from other experienced and knowledgeable people can improve our understanding and fine-tune our decision-making processes. If you see that someone is burning their hand by putting it on fire or jumping off a cliff, you don't have to put your hand on fire or jump off a cliff to know what the consequences would be. You can learn from other people, grow and develop, and ultimately achieve a successful life. First, we should identify those minds in human history, or even in the present time, who are famous for their wise words and contribution to improving life and the human condition. We can learn from them and embrace their lessons. We can live by their words and enhance our way of life. The best lessons are within our reach, and those people can enlighten us.

Humans have a long history, and there are billions of us on the planet who have valuable insights who can share this information with others. For instance, before 500 BC, Gautama Buddha lived a luxurious life as a prince in his early years. He had no worries about where his next meal would come from or the biting cold of a winter night. He had everything and was set to be the king and be well taken care of. However, he was not fulfilled and was suffering. He was in pain, and none of his material possessions could make him happy. In search of enlightenment, Buddha left his luxurious life as he had had enough. However, it didn't take him a day to get out of this rut. He had to search and look deep within, putting in the effort every day. After years of following a spiritual journey and working on his inner self, he reached the pinnacle of his enlightened state and decided to share his experiences with others. The point here is that humans learn lessons from painful experiences and long struggles, but you can learn from them in no time and with ease. You have heard or listened to great stories about people in history who have influenced other people's lives in a positive way, like Prophet Moses, Prophet Jesus, and Prophet Muhammad (PBUH). Another convenient way to find out about other amazing people is through Google. Names, such as Confucius, Leonardo da Vinci, Rumi, Laozi, Galileo Galilei, Isaac Newton, Albert Einstein, and so on, come up as the greatest minds of our time. You can find intelligent minds in the present day, too. My favorite one is Elkhart Tolle, who encourages me to live in the present and, Brian Tracy, whose insights improve my productivity. These people are here to help. Whatever you believe in, from religious sects to atheist ideologies, there's a great mind with helpful tips to living a fulfilled life. But ultimately, the journey starts with you and only you. You determine your success. You determine a peaceful existence. You define the rules. The choice to make a change begins and ends with you. So, what are you waiting for?

Chapter 1

YOU HAVE MORE VALUE
THAN YOU THINK

A t the end of 2013, I became depressed. It was so severe that it caused suicidal thoughts in my mind. I was around 30, and I was completing my post-graduate degree in health economics and management. There were many reasons and factors for my depression, but luckily, one book brought a paradigm shift in my thoughts and changed my perspectives towards life. It saved me from my painful existence and gave me peace of mind. I am thankful to the author. The book is called the *Power of Now* by Eckhart Tolle; I read this book several times. It's difficult to understand because those concepts cannot be understood by the mind only but can be experienced and witnessed in the present through practice. To understand the book, you have to practice it. It took me some time to understand the author's message because I had to practice his technique and read the book repeatedly. The book took me to a place of calmness and enlightenment, helping me to reflect on the value I placed on things and how this affected the decisions I had made in my life. It helped me see the bigger picture and this is why I recommend this book to everyone.

Before discussing why, you are more valuable than you think, I would like to share with you, in this chapter, how this realization happened to me and how my mind produced these positive thoughts. First, I would like to give you some understanding of what needed to change in my life so I could reach this enlightened state. I graduated in the field of nursing with a medical sciences degree and later a postgraduate degree in health economics and management. During these years, I learnt about our global economies and how they relate to our health as beings: global markets, prices, products, their values, and supply and demand. I was about to complete my postgraduate degree, and I wasn't sure what I should do next. I wasn't interested in pursuing a nursing career, but the jobs I was interested in needed many years of experience. Another huge change was that I was entering my thirties, my transformative years. I found myself thinking about issues in a philosophical and rational way. Compared to my twenties, my thirties had taken a drastic turn in my thinking process. I started to think about questions that mattered and thought genuinely about how specific issues in life may affect me. My biggest realization was that we all have great value. We have more value and worth than we think.

There's a straightforward concept in economics that prompted me to think about how you and I or any human in this world have more value than we think and how our true value as human beings is tied to how we see ourselves. Do you ever wonder how a market sets a price for products and how we give importance to that product? We give more value to those products that are more expensive. For example, we give more value to diamonds than water because diamonds are more expensive than water. Simply put, in economics, there are two main factors which affect the price of any product: supply and demand. If there's more supply and less demand, the cost of that product will be low. On the other hand, if there is less supply and more demand, the cost will be high.

One day, a question popped into my mind about what the true values of things are, regardless of market price. In reality, is water more valuable or diamonds? If we compare the value of these two products, according to the market, the diamond is more valuable, but the market price is not absolute because it changes when the supply and demand changes. The market sets a price according to certain conditions. For example, the cost of an umbrella will raise in the rainy season, and it will lower when the rainy season is over. In this case, nobody knows what the true value of an umbrella is aside from the fact that the price changes based on certain weather conditions. So, if we want to know the true value of things, we should remove the condition of the market or set imaginary conditions to solve this problem. For example, if we want to compare the value of water with diamonds, where we have the same amount of supply for both products, then we can deduce the true value of both things and can easily compare and understand which one is more valuable in reality.

Let's imagine we have a new condition in which the supply of water and the supply of diamonds is the same, i.e., we have only one tanker full of water and another full of diamonds in the whole world. Is water more valuable than the diamonds? In this scenario, water is more valuable than diamonds. If we remove the existing market conditions, the true value of water is more than the true value of diamonds because water supports life and life has infinite value. The true values of things are hidden because of market conditions. We are made of 70 percent water. We can survive days without food, but water is essential. Water may be cheap, but in the grand scheme of things, it is precious the same way we humans are precious, too. We are billions on this planet, which creates a condition in where we are unable to understand our true value because of a lack of knowledge or deep understanding of things and their true values. We assume we have nothing unique to offer and end up diminishing our true potential.

The point I want to make here is the market value has also judged humans, and nobody knows the true value of a human being. As a medical student, I knew that one single cell in a human being performs an enormous function even though it is contained in such a tiny space that we can't see it with our bare eyes. Think of a cell as a huge factory and set up in such a small space. I realized the magnitude of a tiny cell after I watched Dr. Najeeb's educational videos on intracellular communication. Dr. Najeeb is a knowledgeable doctor and superb teacher who teaches medical students and has a lot of videos on different medical topics on YouTube. The way he explains things is comprehensive and impressive. He was explaining intracellular communication in such detail that I was lost in my thoughts—in a good way. I was trying to understand the processes associated with intracellular communication like how cells communicate with each other. He took us on a journey, an adventure if you like, explaining how a cell receives a message from other cells and how it generates responses according to the message. I was impressed with his extensive analysis and could visualize his explanations. It is an interdependent chain of cell communication that allows you to breathe subconsciously, to form words, and to feel pain. Just as there are billions of people on the planet, there are trillions of cells in our body that depend on each other. Was this happening randomly? There was no way that all of this was possible without there being a higher power. I had found a new sense of hope in a Creator that molded us from trillions of tiny cells into the various shapes and sizes that we have.

We are made of trillions of these super intelligent cells that all perform specific functions. These cells make different organs, which consequently make beautiful, intelligent bodies. Think about your eyes and how they work and how they look. Eyes introduce us to the colors of the world by merely allowing light into our brain. Our brain detects the different shades of light, allowing us to enjoy different colorful images of beautiful flowers, art gallery paintings, animation films, multi-patterned designs, and beautiful faces. Think about your ears and how they provide a surface for sound vibrations to land, allowing you to hear the sound of a river, the beautiful sound of a cuckoo bird, or the different languages we speak, in which every word carries a meaning. It's a sophisticated system. One of my favorite quotes by Leonardo da Vinci is, "Simplicity is the ultimate sophistication." The movements made by our fingers seem simple, almost mechanical, but if you think about it, you will realize these simple movements require a sophisticated system to enable this movement. At this moment, I am sitting in front of my laptop writing this book. There's a connection between my brain where I am thinking about the words to write down and my fingers that are typing the required words.

Think about how muscles, bones, and neurons work together in such a controlled way and how every cell gets oxygen and nutrients. Think about other organs, which never tire and work 24/7, our hearts pumping blood, gas exchange in our lungs, kidneys filtering our blood, and our gastrointestinal system breaking down food into energy. Our Creator blessed us with such a sophisticated, intelligent, and beautiful body, but we are still not happy with it and feel worthless. We always complain about our looks by saying things like, "My nose is not straight and my teeth are not white enough" or "I am fat or skinny." All we do is complain instead of being grateful. We should ask ourselves why we behave like this and why we always focus on the things we lack instead of focusing on the things we have.

A few years ago, I was watching a video on TED talk by a model named Cameron Russell, who was explaining that good looks aren't everything. She explained that the process of capturing photographs was tiring and demoralizing. She explained that they needed to retake them multiple times, maintaining the same energy throughout, smiling and posing. With huge teams in charge of lighting, makeup, and wardrobes, these photo shoots would take hours, and after these grueling hours, they selected one photo and edited and retouched it to remove any flaws. They needed the image to exude perfection in all areas. The photo would then be placed on billboards for commercial purposes. When an ordinary girl or boy looks at the picture, they may feel inadequate because they don't look like these models, and they aren't aware of the amount of work that has been done. They don't realize that the image of the model has been retouched so many times to epitomize perfection. Cameron explained that Hollywood has single-handedly created self-image problems in teenagers, which will lead them to depression and feeling of worthlessness. Our sense of worth has become tied to the advertising industry's insistence on targeting our disbelief in our value and worth. Hollywood and other beauty-related industries only thrive because there's a demand. A demand fueled by how we view ourselves and our impact on this planet. Think about it this way. If there was no demand, these industries would have no need to supply.

In closing, you are more valuable than a huge tanker full of diamonds because you are a living being. You will realize it when you reflect on your true value and start counting the many valuable gifts blessed to you by Allah. When you muse about these gifts, you will get lost in your thoughts and wonder how you could thank Allah for such infinite valuable gifts. By doing this, you will begin to break away from the traps created by negative thought patterns. This illusion you are trapped in can make you feel worthless and cause irreversible harm. You should always count your blessings whenever you feel down, depressed, or worthless, and you should start reading and thinking deeply to improve your knowledge and understanding of the true value of things. If you want to know the true value of life or being alive, you must read the second chapter (the value of life). After reading it, I believe you will agree with me that you are more valuable than you think.

Chapter 2

WHAT IS THE
VALUE OF LIFE?

One day, I was sitting in my room, consumed by my thoughts. These thoughts revolved around unpacking the true value of life. Is it possible to have a concrete understanding of the true value of life? Can one person know the answer to living a fruitful and enlightened life? Maybe, maybe not. But there are a couple of things that work, and I'd like to share this with you, so listen up. We know we are made of cells, and cells are made of atoms. The chair I am sitting on is also made of atoms. But are we the same? There many differences between this chair and me. I am alive. I am aware of myself. I am aware of this chair. I am aware of this room. I am aware of the world and the whole universe. I witness my existence and the existence of the world. I have emotions and compassion, but this chair, which is also made of atoms, cannot be aware of itself or its surroundings and has no feelings and empathy.

So, a question came to mind. Is it possible to arrange the atoms of this chair in such a way that it also develops the ability to be aware of itself and its surrounding? Suppose we assign this task to the most intelligent scientists and gain funding from the wealthiest people. Is it possible to breathe life into this chair? Let's create an imaginary scenario in which you have a chair in your room, and you love it immensely. You then desire that it comes to life and gains the ability to witness itself, you, and this beautiful world and also have emotions to connect and talk to you. You explain your desire to the most intelligent scientists and the wealthiest people. Suppose those scientists agree to arrange the atoms of the chair in such a way that it will come alive and some of the wealthiest people like Bill Gates agree to fund it. How long do you think it will take for these scientists to achieve this task? How long do you think it will take them to research, prepare, develop and reconstruct this experiment? How long do you think it will take for them, once they put their minds together, to realize your wishes and dreams? And how much do you think it will cost?

Realistically, I think it is impossible for any human being to rearrange chair atoms in such a way that it gains consciousness, even if we spend more than 100 billion dollars. We know it is not possible in reality but let's suppose in our imaginary scenario that one day you receive a phone call from those scientists. After a long struggle and billions of dollars spent, at last, your chair becomes a conscious and is aware of itself and its surroundings. It's gained an emotive response, and you can talk to your chair, too. Now you can get the chance to communicate and build on your friendship. The chair becomes your roommate, and you get to have deep and meaningful conversations with it. However, after a while, you notice that the chair has become depressed. The chair says it now wants to be a bed; it laments that it wants to be as wide as the bed and have its legs further apart from each other. It wants to have a comfortable mattress and be covered by soft and warm blankets. The chair wants to be closer to you and is jealous that you spend more time on the bed and that you enjoy being in bed more than on the chair. You try your best to assure the chair that it is valuable the way it is and that you love and appreciate it. But all this is in vain.

One day, you find the chair has committed suicide and lost consciousness and awareness. How would you feel? You would be sad because you know the chair made a big mistake, especially since you know how much money was spent, how many scientists participated, and how much time it took to breathe life into it. You knew its value, but the chair was not aware of its value. If the chair knew its value, it would never have been depressed and never committed suicide. Allah arranged our atoms in such a way that we have beautiful bodies and we have a lot of capabilities and potential. Being aware of ourselves and our presence in this beautiful world is worth infinite value. What you think of yourself right now is your value, which is limited by your understanding of your abilities and potential.

A few years ago, these thoughts were in my mind. Our Creator has infinite knowledge and wisdom to create such intelligent and beautiful creatures, and the best thing is that He gave us free will to make choices. We are autonomous in our thinking and can think about what we want and bring these ideas to fruition, which makes us autonomous in our actions, too. However, we are always influenced by external pressures—those who are earning or look better than us—causing us to think we have no value. The chair was impressed by the bed and wanted what the bed had. Just like the chair became depressed and suicidal, we become depressed because we compare ourselves to others. We become fixated on things that have a low value. We become obsessed with being like everyone else, instead of looking within to better ourselves. I believe most humans aren't aware of their true value. That's why most of us become so depressed and suicidal. A significant objective of this book is to help you grow and start living with a new perception in which you have infinite value as a human being.

To sum it up, after the realization of the true value of being alive or being a human, you will never have a self-image problem again and never fall into the trap of thinking you are not good enough. Your self-esteem will rise, and you will realize your true potential. This insight will drag you away from the illusion of the mind and will connect you with reality, and you will see beauty and intelligence everywhere. Then you will feel lucky and will experience the joy of life.

Chapter 3

WHAT IS THE VALUE OF MATTER?

When I use the word matter, I am referring to worldly material things that we are fond of accumulating: cars, gold, houses, wealth. Matter or materialism has a different meaning in chemistry and philosophy. In this book, matter means those outer things, which we are always yearning for. The short-term pleasures. Man-made things that give us initial gratification but soon turn into frustration. Those things we spend restless nights thinking about. Those things that cause relationships to break and arguments to occur. I know too well how those things can cause a rift—even within oneself.

In Chapter 1, I talked about meditating, musing, or thinking about how we perceive the value of things and how the state of the market brings equilibrium in product pricing. We already know that the price equilibrium depends on the law of supply and demand. For example, if there is a bigger supply of tomatoes in the market, the price will be low, but if the supply decreases, the price will rise. This rise-fall pattern causes an illusion, which confuses us on what the true value of things are. For me, water is more valuable because it supports life, and diamonds have low value because it has no function within my life. However, this doesn't reflect the current situation.

In the market, diamonds are costly, and water is cheap, so it confuses the nature of things. Doesn't it make more sense for the value of water to be higher than diamonds? This is just one example of how there is a rift in reality and this affects us more than we are aware of. Our decision-making processes are affected in a negative way because we give importance to things according to market prices. We have been duped to believe that market prices represent the true value of things. Maybe duped is not the right word. Let's say we have allowed ourselves to be blinded by our materialistic desires. In reality, the value of things is different. We can make the best decisions in life only when we know the true worth of things instead of giving value to things based on their market prices. Otherwise, we will work hard and will get so far in life but later realize it doesn't even matter. We will think all that matters is having those things that make us feel and look good for the short term. This is what happens every day. To get out of this, we need to think about things differently. We need to restructure our thought processes and reset our priorities.

Years ago, I had a significant dream—the most vivid dream I've ever had—and I still remember it like I had it yesterday. What I saw in that dream was the earth on its orbit in space. Earth looked tiny in space. Then a round coin of five rupees floated within my vision, moving in front of the earth. The earth seemed to disappear as the coin took up space in front of it then my eyes opened. In case you haven't seen a rupee before, five rupees equated to five cents in those days. They looked the same. When I woke up, I thought about this dream and its hidden meaning. The interpretation of this dream is straightforward if we express it in mathematical language. The whole earth is equal to five rupees or less than five rupees because in the dream, it is obscured by the five-rupee coin. In other words, the value of matter is five percent in the universe. Suppose the value of earth is equal to five rupees in reality. How much value does Bill Gates have? Only a few cents or less than that. Or if the value of the earth is equal to five percent, what is the percentage of 100 billion dollars that Bill Gates has? It must be low or even negligible. I was astonished when later I learnt that the percentage of normal matter in the universe, in reality, is five percent or less: the rest is dark energy and dark matter.

This dream freed me from my anxiety and worrying about losing or not having material things, and it worked for me. Let me explain how it worked for me.

In those days, I was broke and had no money. I had no job and needed a bike to look for one, so I borrowed some money from my uncle and bought a bike on lease. After a while, I found a job at a hospital as a staff nurse. My salary was 25 thousand rupees only. The next month, somebody stole my bike from the hospital's parking lot. It cost me a total of 68 thousand rupees so it was valuable for me only if we look at it with the eyes of an ordinary mind. That was a lot of money for me in those days, until I recalled the meaning of my dream. If the whole world is equal to five rupees or five cents, the true value of the bike must be less than a few cents. It looked like I lost nothing, so as I understood that I lost nothing, there was no anxiety in my mind. A fog was lifted, and I still remember how beautiful the sky was because I perceived that I lost something, which was worth less than a cent. However, I would have felt differently if I perceived that I had lost something valuable. I would have been stressed and anxious, which would have caused my health to decline, thus reducing my productivity and creativity. My fruitful and precious days would have been ruined if I had chosen to embrace a warped view and perception of the true value of things.

This dream indicated that the value of matter or materialistic things is only five percent, but it did not indicate what the other 95 percent represents. It could represent life or being alive or being a human because matter is dead, and the opposite of dead is consciousness or being alive. Let's suppose if being alive or being human has a 95 percent value. If we calculate the earth's net worth, which is five percent, it is easy to calculate the other 95 percent value. According to treehugger.com, the net worth of the earth is five quadrillion dollars. How they calculated this is not known, but I will use this figure to illustrate my point. According to the dream, earth is valued at five percent, so now it is easy to calculate because the net worth of the earth is five quadrillion—one percent is equal to one quadrillion dollars, and 95 percent is equal to 95 quadrillion dollars. That means the true value of someone who has nothing—no material wealth—is 95 quadrillion dollars. Now to understand how much one quadrillion is—one quadrillion has 15 zeros, and one trillion has 12 zeros. Just for being alive, your true value is 95,000,000,000,000,000 dollars, and materialistic things are added to it. Those who don't have materialistic things but know their true value are far wealthier than those who have accumulated materialistic things but have no realization of their true worth.

We are 95 percent equal in value. It means we all are extremely valuable, and this realization makes all of us wealthy. According to this dream, those who have more money are not wealthy because their money pales in comparison to life, but on the other hand, those who have the realization of their true value and embrace this aspect of humanity are wealthy. When Steve Jobs was dying, his net worth was 10.2 billion dollars. It is a lot of money, but it couldn't give him another day on this earth. When we have less materialistic things, we feel so miserable because we believe those who have better cars, better homes, and better jobs have more value, based on the emphasis we place on these things. We become depressed and have low self-esteem, which worsens our quality of life. So, first, you should analyze and realize the true value of things that will help you make better decisions and ultimately lead to a better life experience. Being alive is an expensive gift that you should cherish. There are many people today who wish to have one more day with their loved ones and would give up their accumulated possessions to enjoy one more meal. That is the value of life.

It does not mean that we should stop working because money or other materialistic things have no or less value, but it means that life is more valuable than materialistic things. We should do whatever we can to maintain and protect our lives and the lives of our loved ones. If life has a 95 percent value, we have to take care of it and we need some money to maintain our quality of life. As a nurse, I am contributing to society and preserving and protecting the health of others, while earning money to maintain and protect my own life. My primary purpose is not about earning money but to contribute to maintaining life in this world. Everyone can play their role. Whatever your job is, you can make an impact on improving the human condition. If you think you're contributing to society and maintaining life in this world, it will make your job easier, and you will enjoy it because you are doing it for the greater good. I enjoy my duty as a nurse: working night shifts, washing and stitching wounds, and saving people's lives. I never get bored because my primary purpose is not money.

If you are still not convinced that you have already been blessed with a lot of valuable things and are still sad and depressed, yearning for materialistic things, I have a message for you. I can count thousands of things that you have been blessed with and that are more valuable than a billion dollars. The first thing we discussed is life. If someone offers you 100 billion dollars and tells you to kill yourself, will you do that? What if someone offers you 100 billion dollars for both of your eyes, will you accept the offer? Most of us don't realize the true value of health and life and the time we have. I remember a child who was brought to the emergency room and had lung cancer, and he couldn't maintain oxygen saturation because of lung tumors. He had to keep the oxygen mask on at all times. He knew that if the oxygen mask came off for a while, he would die because of a lack of oxygen. Do you ever thank Allah, our Creator, for giving you strong, healthy lungs that can supply your body with oxygen? Or do you ever show gratitude to the Creator for your heart that beats 24/7 and never stops supplying blood to your whole body? Will you exchange your heart for billions of dollars? Do you ever feel gratitude for your brain, which is working for you even when you sleep? Will you exchange it for money? Are you grateful for your learning abilities? Are you thankful that you are educated or that you have caring parents? Are you grateful for your adorable children? Are you thankful for having enjoyable experiences, like being able to take short trips to the mall or taking a walk in the park?

For most people, the little things in life do not matter. Yet, those things equate to the true value of life. My message to you is simple—embrace the new possibility of looking within to find happiness. Start by accepting that it will be difficult to break down the unrealistic expectations that we are exposed to in our day-to-day lives through mediums, such as movies, advertisements, billboards, and even our family and friends. It will be challenging to unpack your deep-rooted assumptions of what is valuable in this life. But it is worth it because you are worth it. You will stand out amongst other people who are stuck in the endless loop of complaining and comparing themselves to each other. You may even lose a few friends because of the positive stance you are taking. You will realize you cannot encourage everyone to change their way of thinking, so focus on you. Adapt a positive mentality and embrace your 95 percent while using the five percent to improve on your 95 percent. You have to be willing to challenge yourself and maintain a grateful attitude.

In sum, the true value of materialistic things is meager compared to life and the experiences you have. We need money to maintain our lives and the lives of our loved ones, and that's why we work. However, our primary purpose should not be to gain material things only but also contribute to society to sustain life for the betterment of the human condition. This is how we can improve our job satisfaction and earn money, and if we lose materialistic things, we should not be aggravated about it. If we worry about losing or not having materialistic things, it will cause stress, which will damage our health in the long run. Your life has infinite value. Remember that.

Chapter 4

FULFILLMENT COMES FROM WITHIN

I'd like to begin this chapter with a short fictional story. A young boy had been searching for a job for two years but couldn't find any. He lived in poverty and for some time, had no money for food. While in his room, he reminisced on the memories he had of his parents who had passed away in a car accident a few years back. He often had flashbacks of the times they spent together, how much they loved and cared for him, and above all, the delicious meals his mother used to prepare. Every day he would look for a job, and at night, he would think about how much he lacked the material things he yearned for. He felt as if luck was not on his side. He became depressed and frustrated, wondering why these terrible things kept happening to him. One night, while in a reverie about the relationship between him and his father when he was a child, he remembered seeing his father doing something in his room. The boy could hear the sound of a hammer on wood. His father was hammering a nail on the boy's bed. The little boy was curious to see what was going on, but his father forbids him from entering the room. As his flashback finished, he was still curious, so he jumped out of bed and started to investigate what the father had done. He flipped the bed upside down and noticed there was a wooden box attached to the underside of the bed. As he detached the wooden box, he found it was full of dollars. When he saw the box full of money, his agony transmuted into ecstasy. He had had money in his room all this time and was feeling hopeless and worthless. It was only after his discovery that he felt like a wealthy man.

Sometimes we look for gratification and satisfaction from outside, but what we need is on the inside and, in most cases, within our grasp. We don't realize we already have it, because our limited vision and lack of understanding causes us to not be aware of it. We are looking for fulfillment in things, which exist outside of us, like cars, money, and status, and even when we get these things, we still don't feel satisfied. We yearn for more and more. If we don't get them, we become depressed and frustrated. But if we stop looking for fulfillment in outside things and focus within to realize our true self (I am or being) or realize the true value of life, we will become fulfilled like the man in the analogy. You can realize your true value when you realize your true self, and this realization will change your state of mind from depression to joy and from feeling unworthy to feeling extremely valuable. So, for those who are looking for fulfillment in low valuable things and have no idea how valuable they are, sooner or later, they will become depressed and frustrated even if they got those things or achieved the goals they desired. External material things may give us short-term happiness, but in the long term, that euphoria will turn into greed—for more things to sustain the temporary feeling. However, it doesn't work like that.

I was shocked when I heard famous American singer, Chester Bennington, committed suicide. He was the lead vocalist for Linkin Park. I googled his net worth, and 30 million dollars was the figure I found, which is a lot of money. Then I searched for images of his family. He had a beautiful wife and six children. I knew how famous he was and his fans loved him a lot, but his suicide shocked me because what an ordinary man would want, he had. I particularly liked one of their songs, which was triggering me to think about the true value of things and prompting me to make better decisions in my life. The lyrics I was thinking about are, "I tried so hard, and got so far. But in the end, it doesn't even matter." What he was talking about in this song was the relationship between time, life, and everyday struggles. I meditate on this song. My analysis of this song is that he achieved the status he wanted through many struggles. He achieved fame, money, and success even though he felt the same on the inside because the happiness he gained from these materialistic things was short-lived. That is why he relayed this message to listeners—that after struggling so hard and spending so much time building and achieving his materialistic goals, it didn't really matter in the end. It means that these things have a meager value in reality. That is why he did not feel fulfilled even after achieving them. His other songs are full of pain too, indicating he was not a happy man. He felt he had no other choice but to commit suicide. Another famous Hollywood actor and comedian, whose suicide influenced and prompted a lot of questions and thoughts in my mind was Robin Williams. I also googled his net worth, and it was $130 million. He also had a wonderful family and had received many Grammy and Golden Globe awards for his acting skills. It astonished me that a man who could make other people laugh, had a 130-million-dollar net worth and a lot of awards was in so much pain that he hung himself. A man who brought such joy to millions of people across the world through his films didn't feel he was worthy enough. He didn't equate his success to being valuable to others.

These examples indicate that money, fame, or family cannot save us from pain, depression, and suicidal thoughts. Put another way, materialistic attitudes don't matter in the grand scheme of things. They don't form the bigger pictures. What matters most in life is life. Let's suppose if the angel of death went to the wealthiest man in the world and said that his time is over and the man replies that he needed more time, but the angel refuses. The man might try to negotiate and bargain because that is what he is used to doing and how he accumulated his wealth. He would ask the grim reaper to take half his wealth and give him one more day to live, but the angel has no use for money and declines. Here, the man will realize the value of having one more day to live is more than everything he has accumulated. In fact, it is worth nothing. At this moment, he might feel poor, and his net worth will mean nothing to him because it cannot save him. It's already happened to Bob Marley, a famous Jamaican singer. When he was fighting for his life due to cancer, he told his son, "Money cannot buy life." It is one of his famous quotes.

Recently, I watched a viral video of a young millionaire named Ali Banat. He recorded a message, and the video went viral after his death. He was diagnosed with stage 4 cancer, and the doctor gave him seven months to live. He sold his successful business and belongings and donated his money to charities based in Africa. He had the Ferrari Spider, priced at $300,000. In another video, an interviewer pointed to his Ferrari Spider and asked him what the value of that car was in his heart? His response was "It's worth one pair of thongs for a little African child with no thongs. It's worth more for me to see him smile with a pair of thongs than any one of these (pointing to his car)." Ali Banat called being diagnosed with cancer a gift because he believed he was given a chance to change himself and have time to prepare to meet Allah on the Day of Judgment. He further said that some people died from a drug overdose in night clubs or died in car accidents and have no time to prepare to meet with the Creator on the day of Resurrection. This painful experience opened his eyes to reality. In another video, he explained that the most valuable thing for him was to wake up in the morning and go to the bathroom using his own feet. Think about this and meditate on it: The most important thing for this millionaire was to wake up in the morning and go to the bathroom using his own feet. Healthy and ordinary people already have this blessing, but they give no value to this because they are stuck in the illusion and give more importance to external things. Having cancer opened Ali's eyes, and he realized the true value of things. For him, fresh air and walking unaided had more value than the Ferrari Spider he had. It costs nothing to breathe in fresh air, but the Ferrari Spider cost him $300,000. That's why he called cancer a gift because it connected him to the reality of the world.

Now I want to tell you the story of another man who had no money, no job, and no fame, but he lived his life full of joy when he realized the true value of self (I am) and connected with reality. He said in an interview that some days he only eats one meal and spends the whole day sitting in a park, full of joy. Nowadays, he is a well-known spiritual teacher and bestselling author of *The Power of Now*, *The New Earth*, and *Stillness Speak*. These books have opened the eyes of millions of people, and I am one of those people. His net worth is more than $70 million, and he is well-known across the globe. Eckhart Tolle found solace and happiness when he had no money, and now that he has plenty of it, he has retained that same sense of gratification. For all intents and purposes, he is swimming in money and has found a way of floating in it. He is happy and fulfilled because he did not identify himself with external things, but he is fully connected within himself. He once said, "I don't have life. I am life." I love this statement because it embodies an enlightened state that many fears embrace. It is a powerful statement because he is saying that life has infinite value, so he also has infinite value.

To conclude, if you crave external pleasures and only work towards getting those needs met, you may get rich, but you'll always feel like something is missing. And because you are obsessed with material things, you will think you need more material possessions to fill in this gap, but that's not how things work. We've seen that this is not the case. Time and time again, the world shows us that material things do not bring a modicum of long-term happiness and a peaceful existence. See the examples of the celebrities I have talked about in this chapter. For most who have had nothing, they may think that having something will make their lives better. Yes, it might, but there needs to be a balance for you to lead a peaceful and joyful existence. In the end, it doesn't matter because fulfillment comes from within. Whenever you realize the true value of life, you will become fulfilled and happy.

Chapter 5

IS PAIN OUR FRIEND OR ENEMY?

Everyone has suffered from pain in their lives, be it physical, emotional or both. As nurses and doctors, we encounter pain in the emergency room frequently. Many patients come to the emergency room with severe pain from issues such as chest pain due to heart attack, kidney stones, and severe trauma, like fractures. Arranging treatment for these physical pains is straightforward. In most cases, giving patient painkillers will cause the pain to dissipate within minutes. We also encounter emotional pain in the emergency room when someone loses their loved one, but we can't apply instant treatment because painkillers do not work on emotional pain. Psychologists can play a positive role by providing counseling to reduce their emotional pain. It then means that one type of pain is more dangerous than the other.

This chapter is about emotional pain. How can we cope with emotional pain with a positive attitude and make it a strength rather than a weakness? Every depressed person has some sort of pain in their lives. If the pain becomes too much to handle and reaches a certain threshold, they attempt suicide. This threshold is different for people and depends on different variables. Those who have been saved are highly likely to attempt suicide again. Why does this happen? Because they can't cope with the pain. I also suffered from extreme emotional pain and having suicidal thoughts but Eckhart Tolle saved me through his book, *The Power of Now*. He provides an in-depth analysis of what emotional pain is, its function, and how it's important for an awakening.

"Everything is created for a purpose," a teacher told me when I was a child, so pain might have an important purpose, too. Pain is a warning call to indicate that there is something wrong and we should do something to fix things. If someone starts feeling severe pain in their flank, they run off to the emergency room to get a diagnosis. After an ultrasound, the doctor can detect that the individual has a kidney stone and advise for either evasive or non-evasive means of treatment. So, what or who has saved that person's kidney and ultimately their life? The pain saved their kidney. If a person's pain receptors are not functioning properly, they would not have detected anything. The brain would send false signals that their body was okay, when in reality, the stones are damaging their kidneys, which could lead to kidney failure. So, yes, pain is our friend and saves us. If we didn't feel pain, we would assume we are okay until it's too late. If we didn't feel anything when we placed our hand on a hot pan, we wouldn't learn that we are burning our hands. Pain has a positive function as it saves our life. However, in our limited understanding, we label it our enemy, so we resist and never accept it. In most cases, our limited understanding of the benefits of pain can lead us into tricky and life-threatening situations. Let's suppose a five-year-old child has a deep cut on his left foot after stepping on glass and is brought to the emergency room. The doctor decides the wound needs to be cleaned, stitched, and dressed. The parents understand that stitches are important, otherwise, the wound will not heal, and the child contracts a serious infection. They understand that this intervention (stitching the wound) is necessary for their child, but the child does not know it because of his limited understanding. The child has no idea what is going on, so he cries and resists. The nurses hold the child's foot tightly, and the doctor gives local anesthesia and starts stitching. The child might think the treatment is brutal and might think the parents are being cruel to stand aside and watch while he is in pain. He may think he is being punished and the adults around him enjoy seeing him suffer. Why does the child resist? He resists because he has limited understanding at the moment that this pain can save his foot. If we put an adult in the same situation, they'll understand that the pain is necessary. They'll accept the temporary inconvenience to save themselves from getting further infections. The adult understands that in some cases, we need to be in pain to get better. The keyword here is getting better. If we wallow in pain for long periods of time, whether physical or emotional, we begin to think that's our new norm and that things will never change and we will always be in pain. But that is not the case.

We have limited understanding of things. As we know, our eyesight has limitations. We cannot see microorganisms with our bare eyes and we can't see very far, so we need equipment to amplify these images. Our ears also have limitations. We can only hear between 20 kilohertz and 20 hertz, but a stethoscope increases this limit. Therefore, our mind is limited in understanding things, but there must be some ways to enhance the understanding level. From the above example, we understand that the actual problem is not the pain but our understanding. Pain has a positive function to save us. Similarly, emotional pain also has a positive function. If someone takes it positively and accepts it, that enhances our awareness and breaks the illusion created by our mind. The more pain we have, the more detached we become from the illusion and can connect to reality, but if someone takes it negatively and resists, it enhances their suffering.

Every successful person has pain in their lives. As the saying goes, "What doesn't kill you makes you stronger." If you research any successful person who has many achievements, they might have gone through some tough times in their lives, too. The more pain, the more the person has achieved. It's as if this pain motivated them to work harder. The question becomes, why do some people commit suicide? My guess would be because they resisted this pain, and instead of embracing and turning it into something positive, they wallowed in the negativity. They thought of the pain as their enemy, and that's why they could not cope. They felt suffocated by the persistent pain and had no tools or understanding of how to get past these negative emotions and to rise like a phoenix from the ashes of negativity. On the other hand, successful people have pain too but they have a positive attitude toward it. They accept it and make the pain their strength to enhance their awareness and utilize their time wisely to attain their goals. They push through until they are successful.

Nobody likes to be in pain because it feels terrible. Failed relationships, being fired, arguments with parents: no one likes to go through those situations. However, by allowing the pain and accepting it, you will be more aware of the present moment. You can roll with the punches and adapt. You gain cat-like reflexes and bounce back from painful situations. In your present state, you will learn quickly how to solve unpleasant circumstances, learn from them, and work through them. That's not to say you will become immune. Far from it. Instead, what will happen is that you now have an understanding of what it takes to solve the painful situation, and when something happens in the future that is worse, you will know how to cope. This positive stance to emotional pain management will radiate high-frequency energy that will attract world-changing thoughts and ideas, which will positively influence your life and lead you to success.

I have explained that pain helps awaken us and improve our awareness and lead us to the path of success. It means that pain makes us stronger. As we know, pain is an unpleasant sensation, and its experience sometimes disturbs our daily routine and decreases our productivity. Sometimes the pain produces suicidal thoughts. So what should we do to reduce the intensity of the pain and revert back to our daily routine? First of all, we should accept the pain, witness its presence, and acknowledge the thoughts related to it. Then we should analyze the problem which caused the pain to decipher the nature and degree of the problem. Sometimes there isn't a realistic problem but a created one. If someone perceives that their partner is cheating on them, but in reality, they are not, this perceived situation causes pain. In this case, they've made a mountain out of a non-existent molehill.

One day, I heard a story about a female patient who had been brutally murdered by her husband. One of our male nursing staff was from the same village where this murder had happened, and he knew the murderer because they lived close to each other. He told me that her husband was suffering from some mental health issue—schizophrenia or paranoid personality—and was also addicted to marijuana. According to research, those who use marijuana are more prone to paranoid episodes. Because his mental issues were undiagnosed, the murderer perceived that his wife was cheating on him, and he killed her. He had no understanding that his mental health issues may be exacerbated by consuming an illicit drug. Instead of getting the help he needed, he gave into these misdirected assumptions and took the life of another. If he had been diagnosed, perhaps the illness could have been managed, and his wife would be alive today.

Another sad story is about one of my fellow classmates who failed his matric exams after two attempts. He committed suicide shortly after. He might have passed it on his third or fourth attempt, but we will never know. Many rich and successful people dropped out of school, but they continuously worked. My friend's warped perception of his situation led to his death and he failed to realize that you don't have to go to school to be successful. He lost his life, which has infinite value. Whatever the reason for your painful life situations, you should analyze it and weigh the various possibilities.

Most of the people brought into the emergency room for committing suicide was because a relationship has failed or their partner is cheating on them. I still remember the case of a young man who committed suicide for a minor reason. He was 25 years old and took a wheat pill, which is a strong poison that has a minimal survival rate. In the beginning, he was conscious and was able to talk, and I asked him why he took the poison. He replied that he couldn't work because he had problems with his spine, but people thought he was lying and making excuses. It's unbelievable that someone would commit suicide for such a small issue. He died in front of his parents. It was an extremely sad moment for me because he was so young. The man had perceived his issue to be serious and had overreacted to other people's responses to his unemployment.

A young woman from Pakistan named Muniba Mazari is now a motivational speaker, and she shared her story in a forum in Malaysia in 2017. She said she had a severe car accident with her husband, had multiple fractures and was unconscious for a few days as a result. After regaining consciousness, she learnt she will never walk again because her spine was shattered and had lost control of her lower body. Later, a doctor told her she will never become a mother because the accident had destroyed her uterus. Muniba explained that this was the worst news for her. She had been bedridden for two years and explained how lucky other people are because they can walk and go outside, but they aren't even aware of it. She further explained that after being placed in a wheelchair for the first time, after two years of being bedridden, she was happy. She considered herself reborn on that day and celebrated. Even with this blessing, she found herself sinking into external pressures once again. The first-time applying lipstick, she found herself looking in the mirror and wondering what other people would think. She shook herself from these thoughts and applied another layer of lipstick, this time focusing on herself. She had reached a point where what others thought of and about her did not matter anymore. Then she said she worked on her fears.

The biggest fear Muniba had was her impending divorce, so she realized that it was nothing but a fear in her mind. This realization made her emotionally strong. With a smile, she explained that she texted good wishes to her husband on his new marriage. Her next fear was being unable to give birth, so she adopted a son. Her final fear was facing people. She built her self-confidence and is now a motivational speaker. She has gone through a lot, and her approach to analyzing her problems has led to her prominence and success. She embraced the pain as a friend because she learnt a lot during her painful situation, and now she is successful and fulfilled. You see, most of our perceived issues are attached to our egos. Muniba could have easily chosen to be sad that she couldn't walk anymore, that people would look down on her, that her divorce meant she is unworthy of love, and that she could not have a child. She could have given up and given into these negative thoughts. She could have given into the pain and trauma of being confined to a wheelchair. The pain that her husband, who had vowed to be with her through sickness and in health now wanted nothing to do with her, was married to someone else. But she chose a different path, kicked her ego aside and focused on healthy ways to make her life worthwhile.

Another example is from the movie, *Forrest Gump*, which is one of my favorite movies. Tom Hanks plays the character of Forrest Gump, who is an American soldier. Forrest enlisted and shipped to Vietnam during the war under the supervision of Lieutenant Dan. Forrest felt lucky working under Lieutenant Dan because "he was from a long and great military tradition. Somebody from his family had fought and died in every single American war." In one scene, they were attacked by Vietnamese soldiers in the jungle. Forrest's friends were badly injured, and some died. Forrest was trying to save his injured friends by carrying them out of the jungle to a safe place. He saw that Lieutenant Dan also badly injured and tried to save him, but Lieutenant Dan wanted to die in the field like his ancestors. Forrest carried him from the jungle and saved his life. When the war was over, Forrest was awarded the Medal of Honor for his bravery and valor and for saving the lives of his fellow soldiers. Unfortunately, Lieutenant Dan's injuries were severe, and he ended up losing both his legs. Lieutenant Dan was angry with Forrest because he wanted to die in the field with honor and dignity, but then he had no legs to use. He was suffering from both physical and emotional pain, but later in the movie, Lieutenant Dan gained a peace of mind and realized that life is also beautiful even without legs. The moral of the story is that nothing is more precious than life. If you are alive, you are a lucky person, so we should be grateful every time. Gratitude is the best way to decrease the pain and develop a positive attitude towards life. The best blessings in our lives are to be alive. If you are alive and depressed, you are the luckiest unlucky person in the world. However, it doesn't make sense to be the luckiest unlucky person.

You need to choose one. Choose to be lucky and blessed.

To summarize, pain can be our enemy if we resist and perceive it as negative. It can play the role of the villain in our story and can damage us, but in contrast, the pain can be our friend if we accept, surrender, and use it as a source of strength. It can help in building our awareness, learning, and teaching us to never give up. Pain can play the role of the hero in our lives and help us to be the best that we can be.

Chapter 6

OUR ABILITY TO LEARN

In the Adam and Eve creation story from the Quran, Allah said to the angels, "Verily, I am going to place mankind generations after generations on earth." They said, "Will You place therein those who will make mischief therein and shed blood, while we glorify You with praises and thanks and sanctify You." Allah said, "I know that which you do not know." (Quran 2:30) "He taught Adam all the names of everything" (Quran 2:31). Allah imbued Adam with an insatiable need for and love of knowledge. After Adam had learned the names and uses for all things, Allah said to the Angels, "Tell me the names of these if you are truthful." They answered, "Glory be to You, we have no knowledge except what You have taught us. Verily it is You the All Knower, the All Wise" (Quran 2:31-32). God turned to Adam and said, "O Adam! Inform them of their names," and when he had informed them of their names, He said, "Did I not tell you that I know the unseen in the heavens and the earth, and I know what you reveal and what you have been hiding?" (Quran 2:33). I mention this story because this helped me to develop an important insight, which is Allah blessed us with the ability to learn. Allah is proud of us because of this learning ability, and that's the only reason, in my opinion, which makes humans the best creature. I was unaware of my ability to learn until my thirties, so I did not use it consciously and did not benefit from it much. One day, I realized or discovered my learning abilities, and after that day, my life change.

Now I will share my story of how I developed this insight and how it helped me. I was a timid person in my class, so I participated very little in classroom discussions, and the most challenging thing for me was the presentation aspect because of low confidence. I also did not do well on exams and was hardly getting the grades needed to graduate. But somehow, I finished nursing school. However, I still struggled with my practical skills. When I started my job as a staff nurse in an emergency room, I was having a tough time, and my manager and supervisor were not happy with me. After 10 months, I received a termination letter from human resources. I was flummoxed at that time and had mixed feelings about it. I was happy because I got rid of a tough job in the emergency room, but at the same time, I had no idea what to do next. After wasting one year, I enrolled in a postgraduate program called health economics and management. After finishing this program, I thought I would find a better job in the public health sector. This was an escape plan from a nursing career. I was criticized by people, especially in my family, at that time. According to them, I should have done a postgraduate degree in nursing, but I was trying to escape from the nursing field.

After completing the program, I could not find a job with my master's degree because the advertised positions required many years of experience, which I did not have. I was bewildered and depressed and did not know what to do next. I had no money, so I borrowed some money from friends to make ends meet. Those were the days when I was reading spiritual books like *The Power of Now*, *The Alchemist*, *The Four Agreements*, *The Celestine Prophecy*, and some other books by Deepak Chopra. These books helped me to cope with depression and expanded my understanding of the world around me. I learnt from one of Deepak Chopra's books about what intuition is and how it works. Intuition is a strong feeling without logical or rational thoughts. It helps in decision-making and leads us to our destiny. After reading these spiritual books, I got an intuition that I should pursue my nursing career, and I had a strong instinctual feeling to get back into nursing. It was a paradigm shift in my mind because I began to enjoy the idea of being a nurse. My mindset had changed, and I began envisioning myself helping those in need. So, I followed my intuition, and I chose a nursing career consciously and jumped back into it. However, I had a challenge ahead of me because what I learned in nursing school and during the 10 months, I worked in the emergency room had evaporated from my mind completely. I made a plan that I would refresh my knowledge again and find a nursing job at a hospital. Those days, I was also practicing techniques learnt from those spiritual books, especially from *The Power of Now*. By practicing these techniques—surrender, mindfulness, gratitude, focusing on the present, focusing on space and silence, and being attentive to our inner souls—my mind's eye became open to another dimension of life, and my agony transmuted into joy. Externally, people perceived me as a loser because I didn't have a job or achievements as compared to my friends and classmates.

To find a job, I needed a bike to visit different hospitals, so I borrowed some money from my maternal uncle to buy a bike on lease. I bought one and started practicing how to ride a it because I was an amateur bike rider, and in the beginning, I felt anxious riding on highways. One day, while searching for a job, my mind latched onto this question: "Will I be able to ride a bike without being anxious on the busy highways?" This question kept popping in and out of my mind. The relevancy of this experience will become clearer later on. After a few months of struggling to find a job, with the help of a friend, I found one in the emergency room at a hospital once again. I was thrilled to find a new job, and when I was going back to my residency on that bike, I noticed that after three months, my bike riding skills had improved and that I was riding without any anxiety. The nagging question kept coming back to me. I had learnt how to ride the bike, and therefore, I knew I could learn other things, too. My belief was so strong that if I wanted to learn about rocket science, I could, so I decided I would use my learning abilities to improve my nursing skills and knowledge. I downloaded some nursing books and started watching videos of nursing skills on YouTube, and after one year, I had improved considerably.

In those days, I also practiced living in the present moment. I was finally enjoying life, and my understanding of the power of knowledge filled me with joy. It was as if I was seeing things for the first time in my life. Whenever I looked to the sky, it was more beautiful than ever before. If I looked at a flower, it looked so alive and attractive. I was noticing details everywhere I looked as my eyes were open and receptive to all the beauty surrounding me. Most of my friends were earning higher salaries than me and getting married. They thought I was a failure, but they judged me based on my external appearance and surroundings but did not know about the joy of being in the present. I worked at that job for 17 months until I took a test in international NGO MSF. I passed the test and was selected as an emergency room staff nurse once again. My salary increased two-fold, and I found a better team to work with. That was a busy emergency room, but they have a good setup. There were also some ex-pats working from different countries, like Canada, Australia, and South Africa. I had that strong belief yet that I could learn, so I kept learning and practicing those skills I needed to improve. I attended and completed different trainings, and after two years of working with MSF, I improved my skills and knowledge to a competent level, and I became more confident and had no anxiety or panic attacks. After three years, on May 2019, I applied for a job in the government sector in Pakistan, and I was selected to interview as a nursing lecturer at the Mardan College of Nursing. My salary increased four-fold as compared to my first salary, and my nursing skills and knowledge improved to expert level in five years. This realization that I had the ability to learn brought a positive change in my life, and now I can learn how to teach these skills and knowledge to my students.

As a human, I feel grateful for the ability to learn because it gives me confidence and reduces the perceived external pressures of life. My quality of life has improved. I want to utilize my learning abilities to the fullest capacity, so I started learning other things which could help me in my life, like self-defense techniques, defensive driving, chess, writing, and interpersonal communication. Our mind is like an operating system or window of a computer. We can download any app into it. For self-defense, I started learning about martial arts. Martial arts have many benefits. If you practice it, you will burn calories, meaning you are exercising, keeping your body in good shape, and preventing diseases. Another advantage is that it helps you to survive life-threatening situations. It can save your life or the life of your loved ones. It's not necessary to have a black belt, but we should learn some self-defense techniques to protect ourselves from bullies or insanely aggressive people. YouTube is my greatest teacher. I review different martial arts types, such as kung fu, boxing, MMA, jujitsu, and some others. I learnt a few self-defense techniques, which will be helpful in any potential life-threatening situation and also boosts my confidence. I also learnt how to play chess. In four months, I improved my rating score from 0 to 1400. Now, it is like I am an advanced beginner in chess, and if I continue, I will become a strong player because I have the ability to learn. If I apply myself every day even a little, in five years, I will become a competent player. I also improved my driving skills. Before this insight, I was a bad driver, but now I am a good driver and driving confidently; I can now parallel park easily. I also learnt some productivity tactics from well-known author, Brian Tracy. I am working on my writing skills—writing this book would have been impossible without developing this insight.

I can learn things because I am a human, so I have the ability to learn. I read a beautiful sentence in a management book that said, "We can learn anything, but we can't learn everything," meaning it is hard to learn all languages or all sports. Knowledge and skills are infinite, so you should learn from those who can help you in your life and job. It's up to you what you want to learn. You can learn anything, but it may take time and one day you will become an expert if you don't give up. I believe you can even learn rocket science, politics, singing, writing, cooking, and any sport because humans have infinite potential and should use it consciously. If someone believes that they have a low IQ and make excuses that learning is hard, they might take a little more time than the one who has a higher IQ, but the important thing is that you can learn. It's not about how quick you can learn because achieving goals is making the difference even if it takes time.

Here's an analogy for you. You might observe a heavy loaded truck moving toward you slowly on an inclined road. You may see the driver struggling with the clutch. You may see traffic piling up behind it and people honking for the truck to move faster. Even though it's moving slowly, it will reach its destination. You will also observe that despite people honking, they will remain a few meters away and give the truck some space. What can we learn from this? Keep moving! You should always move towards your goal. No matter how slowly or disheartening it may seem, take your time and gain the knowledge you need. Then keep moving.

Some people have locked up their learning abilities and have developed the belief that they cannot learn. One of our watchmen has such a lock to his learning ability. One day, he brought his phone to me and showed me a text that someone had sent him and asked me what was in this text. He couldn't read. He said he was weak in school, so he quit. He further said that his children were going to school and they could read, so I tried to encourage him to improve his reading by telling him that if his children could do it, he could, too. I even mentioned that YouTube could help him learn how to read. I tried to show him how to flick through different videos to learn about reading, but he did not seem interested. He did not want to unlock his learning ability because his belief was so strong that he couldn't learn. A beautiful quote by Brian Tracy says, "Whatever you believe with feeling becomes your reality." The consequences for not unlocking his learning abilities is that he will make no progress in his life.

If you want to make progress in your life, you need to learn new skills and gain knowledge by unlocking your abilities; so start learning new things and build your learning muscles. Building learning muscles is similar to building body muscles. To build your body, you need to go to the gym and exercise. When someone new joins the gym, they observe a lot of people exercising and lifting heavy weights with great stamina. They might be intimidated by this in the beginning. For the newcomer, exercising is difficult and makes them tired so they can't even lift a light weight as compared to others. Seasoned gym goers are better than newcomers because they have already developed their bodies; however, they possibly faced the same problems when they first started too. If newcomers continue their exercises, they will be able to lift heavier weights and have an increased stamina. The same principle applies to learning, too. At the beginning, you might have some problems, but if you don't give up and continue learning, one day, you will become an expert.

Another benefit of learning new things is that it also reduces levels of stress, anxiety, and depression because the mind diverts from negative thoughts. Learning new things involves maintaining a positive mindset. As you start learning new things, your mind is unable to produce negative and destructive thoughts because you have engaged your mind in learning. For example, if you want to learn how to sing, your mind is focused on singing, and any problems will be diverted. While learning something new, any negative thought patterns that you had acquired before or had become a habit will be broke, and your reward center will be activated, moving you one step closer to your goals.

To sum up, I believe every human has the ability to learn and can learn anything they want. These new skills and the knowledge they have gained can bring a positive change in their lives for the better. I believe that every human has the ability to learn, and now it's up to you. It really is that simple. Learning equates to a positive mindset, which equates to a peaceful existence. One course of action affects the other.

Chapter 7

LEARNING FROM OTHERS.

During my journey of enlightenment, I was thinking about Eric Erickson's psychosocial developmental theory, which I had learnt in my graduate program in nursing. The theory suggests that every human being passes eight stages of life and every stage has its own psychosocial crisis. The first stage is infancy between 0 to 18 months, and in this stage, the psychosocial crisis is trust versus mistrust. It means that if an infant's needs are fulfilled on time, they will develop trust. On the other hand, if their parents fail to take care of the baby, the baby begins to mistrust their intentions. The second stage begins when infants become toddlers, between two to five years. Now they face a new psychosocial crisis, which is autonomy versus inferiority. If parents let the toddler perform tasks, such as putting on their shoes and tying their laces, the toddler will develop autonomy. If the parents continue to provide for the child as if they were an infant, the toddler will have a stunted psychosocial response as they become older. The third stage is the preschool stage when toddlers become young children between five to eight years. In this stage, the young child goes through the initiative versus guilt crisis. Here, they learn the concept of right and wrong, and the consequences involved. They begin to develop their personality and start to build on their characters. These stages are crucial in our lives. We all know that children imitate what they experience. They learn the difference between good and bad and right and wrong from the people around them. Therefore, if they have bad experiences, this sticks with them and dictates how the rest of the stages play out.

The fourth stage between 8 to 11 years is the prepubescent stage when young children become young teens. The psychosocial crisis is industry versus inferiority. Young teens begin to learn where they fit in or where society tells them they fit in. There's immense pressure to fit in at this stage, and young teens begin to realize that to be acknowledged and praised, they need to conform—going to school, getting good grades, doing the household chores, and so on. For some teens, they begin to feel the pressure of being fit into a box and lash out. In the fifth stage, between 11 to 19 years, is the adolescent stage, and the crisis is identity versus role confusion. The young teens have become hormonal teenagers. Their bodies are growing, and they are realizing that more responsibility is required of them. If all other stages have been encountered and managed well, the teenagers will adapt at this level. However, due to peer influence and the need to fit in, some teenagers may find themselves in life-threatening situations because "their friend said it's okay." This is the stage we learn self-control and how to manage our feelings appropriately.

The sixth stage is the adult stage, usually between 20 to 35 years. The psychosocial crisis is intimacy versus isolation. It is important to note that in the sixth stage, progression becomes longer, and things are changing during these years. For example, you may have started university when you were 20, graduated when you were 24, got your first permanent job when you were 26, got married when you were 28, had your first child when you were 29, and bought your first house when you were 32. I'm sure you get the gist. At each of these points, something is happening, and a change is occurring in your life. The seventh stage is the middle age between 35 to 50 years, and the psychosocial crisis is generativity versus stagnation. You've heard of men going through a midlife crisis when they buy all the materialistic things they've always wanted and, in some cases, get divorced and marry a young woman. At this stage, people go through a transformative experience. Children are off to college, and the adult is nearing retirement age. It brings forth a lot of feelings about getting older and what that means. The last stage occurs between 50 years to death, and the psychosocial crisis is integrity versus despair. This is the stage where people reflect back on their lives. If the psychosocial crisis in their lives were handled appropriately, which is rarely the case because we are inherently imperfect, then the individual will look back with no regrets. However, due to our flawed nature, we make mistakes along the way. And that is fine as long as we learn from them and move on.

Every psychosocial stage has different and unique challenges. At the beginning of every new stage, the person is a novice to those psychosocial challenges. We know very little, but as we grow up, we accumulate experiences and life lessons. Towards the end, we have more knowledge. I was in my thirties when things were falling apart for me, so I was between the fifth and sixth stages. My knowledge and experiences couldn't match those who were in the later stages, so I could learn from them and their experiences and prepare myself for future challenges. These thoughts helped me realize that learning from other experienced and knowledgeable humans would be beneficial to me.

Learning from other intellectuals is a good strategic move because their knowledge is readily available.

From Buddha, I learnt the art of mindfulness. Being mindful means that one doesn't judge others or situations outrightly but experiences issues in the present. This helps to improve the awareness of your thoughts and emotions and connects us to reality. Practicing mindfulness leads us to a state of mind, which can produce high quality thoughts and experiences based on reality. Simply put, we can improve our mind functionality and gain clarity in our desired goals. When we judge a thing as beautiful, our mind makes it more appealing, and it becomes an illusion.

There is a beautiful quote by Anais Nin that says, "We don't see things as they are, we see them as we are," meaning we don't see reality, but we see things or people as our mind labels them. This reminds me of an incident from my childhood. My elder brother took me to the market to buy me a pair of shoes. I saw one black pair of shoes, which I liked, but my brother disapproved. He took me to another shop, but I didn't like any that were on display, especially since I had already made up my mind about which pair I liked. After searching through a couple more shops and being adamant that none of the shoes were like the first pair we saw, my brother frustratedly bought the initial pair. I was ecstatic, but after the euphoria wore off the next day, the shoes didn't look as appealing as they did in the shop. They looked different to me.

They had lost their shine. I didn't understand why at the time, but now I understand that in the shop, my mind labelled it as appealing and made me want them. So, when we see things, we label them according to our preferences. To see things as they are, we should practice the art of mindfulness, which helps break the mind's created illusion and connect us to reality.

The point is that I learnt this technique of mindfulness from Buddha quite easily, but Buddha himself learnt it the hard way through the struggles in his life. He left his family, lived in the jungle, and meditated for several years. I can only imagine what he must have faced, particularly criticism because of his background—he was a prince—and his father and wife must have had different expectations for him. But for him, something needed to change. After several years, he reached his enlightened state and decided to share with the world what he had learnt. Michael H. Hart ranked him fourth in his book, *The 100: A Ranking of the Most Influential Persons in History.* Sometimes we need to learn from others to avoid making mistakes. You may think it's a cowardly move, but, if it's evident that the outcome will be a negative one, avoid it.

Humans have an intellectual mind and can learn things from others' mistakes and experiences. Nowadays it's very easy to light a fire, but you can imagine in the early days, someone had to discover and practice how to light a fire. I'm sure there were a few accidents that led to loss of human life due to poor fire control. Thankfully, we have modified how our ancestors used to perform certain functions and a century from now, our inventions today will be obsolete. Considering the number of people on this planet, one problem can have a variety of angles and consequences. People can have different points of views on how to tackle an issue. There are a lot of books to read and to learn from and improve our quality of life. Those who are 70 years old and above have gone through all the psychosocial stages of life. They've loved, and they've lost. They've been fired and hired, depressed then enlightened, and have had friends pass away and grandchildren born. People have bought houses and lost them. They experienced all that life has to offer. So, it only makes sense to learn from them and to drink from their pool of knowledge. Of course, some care is required as we've discussed. There may be some individuals who haven't managed each stage appropriately and are stuck in an endless loop of negativity. Caution must be applied, but if the information is steeped in positivity, "Use, reuse, and recycle."

In my opinion, there are two ways of acquiring knowledge. One way is to learn from one's own experiences, which is a hard way, and another way is to read books or any other medium that you may prefer. Holy books are full of knowledge and guidance with messages directly from the Creator. These books are authentic guides or manuals for how to live our lives. These books work like a light piercing through the darkness, but we have made them controversial sources of information because we have separated ourselves into different sects, with each sect having their own holy book. I think everyone should read all these holy books if they want to understand life and one's purpose and aims on this planet. We should take guidance from them.

There are other kinds of books which are produced by human minds reflecting their life experiences or by researching on different topics. If someone wants to improve their job performance and achieve success in their career, wants to improve their business acumen and wants to learn new ways to be more efficient and effective, they can get a book to guide them through these paths. There are many books written on how to be successful in one's career, how to develop a new business or ways to earn passive income or improve your quality of life. Many intellectuals have studied successful people and the techniques and tactics they have used to create, maintain, and navigate a successful life and are sharing this research through books. My favorite among them is Brian Tracy, American-Canadian motivational public speaker and self-development author. He has written more than 70 books. I remember from one of his videos on YouTube that he writes one book in 90 days. He said that every skill is learnable, so he reads books on a variety of topics and writes about them. He said that if one man can do it, another man can do it, too. If he can write four books in a year, you can write at least one book in a year. He inspired me to write this book. Another classic book is *Think And Grow Rich* by Napoleon Hill. He interviewed hundreds of successful people to understand the secrets behind their success and shared this information with us through the book, which is among the 10 bestselling self-help books of all time. These books and other helpful material are a quick search away. The power of technology has made our lives so much easier, and yet, we still complain.

If you are interested in the universe and want to know how the stars align or how many kilometers Earth is away from the sun, there are numerous books on the topic—even animation guides. If you are curious about the voyage of human understanding through science, Karl Sagan is the man to look up. He directed a documentary called *Cosmos*, which tracks the development of the universe in a chronological order from the beginning until the 21st century. This documentary explains atoms and galaxies and how everything relates to each other. It helped me to expand my understanding about the universe and how vast it is.

There are a lot of great minds we can learn from. Learning from others is beneficial and straightforward, and you can start with Hart's book, *the 100: A Ranking of the Most Influential Persons in History,* where you can get an idea of the world's greatest minds and the books/material you should read. These are just a few examples. Every second, a great mind is born, and we owe it to ourselves to learn from them. So, the moral of the story is that a wise person is someone who continues to learn whether they learn from their mistakes or learn from more experienced people. There's a lot of guidance readily available in the world that can help you improve your quality of life and help you build and live a peaceful, worthwhile existence.

Chapter 8

BELIEVING IN YOURSELF

The secret ingredient to success is to believe in yourself. I've heard this statement several times before, but I had no idea what it meant until I realized the deeper meaning. I would like to share how that realization came to me. I developed this insight in my early thirties when I used to spend time watching movies during my days off from work. The movie from which I learnt that we cannot be successful in life until we believe in ourselves is *Kung Fu Panda*, which is an animated movie based on Eastern philosophy or ancient knowledge of China. There are a lot of valuable messages for the audience, but the message or lesson which inspired me will be discussed in this chapter. First, we should understand the background of some characters to understand the messages better. In the movie, there is a big panda named Po, who is chosen as dragon warrior by the master Oogway. Po learns all the skills he needs to be a dragon warrior except for the final step. This step is crucial for him to restore peace in his community. The secret to the last step is written in a dragon scroll.

Once he completes all the steps, his master gives him the scroll, but Po is shocked after he opens the dragon scroll because it is blank. Po can only see the reflection of his face. He does not understand and becomes disappointed. He feels he has been duped and that all his training has built up to nothing. You see, he has built this expectation in his mind of the secret held within the scroll, thinking it hides some unknown treasure. He leaves the Jade Palace, where he has been trained and goes back to his father's noodle shop. His father tries to convince him to go back and fulfil his duty and tries to offer up the tightly held secret to his special noodle soup, famous in their community, Peace Valley. Po sits still, waiting to be told what it was. His father confesses that there was no secret ingredient and that if you believed the soup is special, it became special. Po realizes that the secret ingredient is nothing but believing in oneself. After he develops this belief that he is unique, he defeats Ti Lung, who is the villain that wants to attack Peace Valley for the dragon scroll.

It may have been an animation for children, but the message is loud and clear—if you don't believe in yourself, you can't be successful. So, the secret ingredient to your success is you, and the secret ingredient to mine, is me. If you want to become successful, only you can make it happen, and you have to believe in yourself. Some people might not understand it yet. Some people have become dependent on others, so much so, that they can't see themselves living without the other. This happens all the time in relationships when you become a parent and even when you work at a company for a long time. Your life becomes tied up, and you don't know how to break free from the illusion. You may want to start a business after your children have left the nest or when you are fired. Usually, this takes time because people have been dependent on others to motivate them and push them forward, but now it has come a point where you need to believe in yourself and fulfil your heart's desires.

We are all different in one way or another. Let's take the example of fingerprints. No one in the world has identical fingerprints. Out of the seven billion people on earth, not one person has the same fingerprint. Why is that? Scientists have reported that during conception, parents' gametes make a zygote, which turns into a different code of DNA. Our DNA is 99.9 percent identical, and what makes us unique is nearly 0.1 percent of our genome. This may seem insignificant, but the human genome is made up of three billion base pairs, which means 0.1 percent is still equal to three million base pairs. Those three million different base pairs make us unique and special. If you still believe that 0.1 percent difference is not sufficient enough and if you watch the *Cosmos* documentary by Karl Sagan, you'll understand that in comparison to the universe, our planet is minuscule, like a speck of dust. But to us, our planet is big, so 0.1 percent difference in our genome is enough to make us unique and special. If you are unique and special, you must have some unique abilities and can do something that is unique to you. We also share 99.9 percent DNA with other humans. It means that if one human can do something, so can you. If Bill Gates can earn that much money, you can earn it. If Messi can play football the way he does, you can play, too. If Eminem can rap and Rihanna can sing, you can rap and sing, too. If Brian Tracy can write a lot of books, you can do it as well. If one human can do one thing, you can do it because we share 99.9 percent of our DNA.

Another reason you should believe in yourself is to think about your Creator. You are created by the all-mighty Creator, Allah. Think about his great design. If you Google the diameter of the observable universe, you will be astonished how huge this universe is. The diameter of the observable universe is 93 billion light years—one light year is the distance covered by light in one year. Light can travel eight times around the earth in one second. So, when light travels for one year, it's called one light year. Think how much distance it will cover in kilometers. Imagine the diameter of 93 billion light years and how much distance that is. It's beyond our imagination. Now you have a clue how big the observable universe is. We are created by the same Creator who designed such a huge universe, and you are the best creature the Creator molded, now you can imagine how much potential you have. Every human on the planet has infinite potential, and it's up to us to unlock our potential and be successful. Oprah Winfrey says it best in this quote, "You become what you believe." This is the secret ingredient to success. If you believe in yourself, you can learn and can do anything.

To strengthen your belief in yourself, you should read about the potential of the human body and mind or its mechanics or how it is designed. Watch different educational documentaries and read material about us and think about your own body and how it functions. Think about the fact that we have trillions of cells, and each tiny cell has a blood supply and gets nourished. Think about your brain made of 100 billion neurons, and these 100 billion neurons are making trillions of synapses and connections. Study the functions of a cell, how these cells communicate, and how our immune system protects these cells. Just as the universe has billions of galaxies, you have trillions of cells. You are a universe by yourself, and you have infinite potential. Still, there is a lot to explore when it comes to human potential. Keep yourself updated with new research on the human body, mind, and its functionality.

To summarize this chapter, believe in yourself. Believe in your capability to make sound decisions. Take the initiative. Challenge yourself to achieve your goals. Have autonomy over your mind and it will transform you into an independent thinker, and you will take responsibility for your life and won't care what other people think. You will decide for yourself because you believe in yourself. Not every decision will be the right one, and if you end up making a mistake, learn from it and rise. Give yourself credit for trying and move past this bump in the road. Strive to be mindful of your well-being and those around you. Clear your mind and relax your soul. Say goodbye to anxiety and depression and any other negative thoughts or habits. We can never be successful without this secret ingredient. The secret is you, and you have limitless potential to activate what you need to create, maintain, and navigate a peaceful existence.

Chapter 9

THE CREATOR

We know that nothing travels faster than light in the universe with a speed of 299,700 kilometer per second. Let's do a bit of math here. It takes one second from the moon to the earth and eight minutes from the sun to the earth. The distance between the sun and earth is 149.6 million kilometers. The distance covered by light in one year is called one light year. If we convert one light year to kilometers, it becomes 10 trillion kilometers. The nearest galaxy to us is almost two million light years away, and the diameter of the observable universe is 93 billion light years. This means that we receive light from that far. I'm sure in a few years some scientists will develop technology that will allow us to see further into the universe. We live in such a vast universe, which is hard to imagine. The point here is that the way our universe is significant cannot be matched with how powerful and intelligent our Creator is.

Now let's talk about the small things. Do you ever wonder how small our human cell is? It is almost 0.05 millimeter in diameter. It's smaller than the dot of the ballpoint pen, which is 0.7 millimeter. In such a small 0.05-millimeter space, there is a huge factory, which performs complicated tasks, and they continuously replicate themselves. Every cell has DNA, which is like an instructional book for the cells. These instructions determine a number of factors. Some of us have blue eyes, and some have brown. Some have curly hair, and others, straight hair. Some are fair-skinned, while others are dark. All these variations are because of the different instructions within the DNA. The Creator put the instruction book (DNA) in such a small space, even smaller than a ballpoint dot. If we convert these instructions to physical books, it would fill one million pages or 5000 books. My point is simple. All these complex processes did not just happen; it was at the hands of our Creator. If a physical book cannot be written without an author, then our cellular structures did not just occur. Our Creator formed a marvelous universe, full of beautiful things that we are yet to discover, including our hidden potential. We have been exploring our universe for thousands of years, and we are still inventing new technologies to discover new dimensions and aspects. Five hundred years ago, Galileo invented the first telescope, observed planets, and confirmed the heliocentric modal of our solar system. In present day, we can see through modern advanced telescopes 93 billion light years away. Can you imagine what we will have discovered 500 years from now?

The concept of the infinity is present not only in the vastness of the universe but also in a fundamental particle of the matter. Two thousand five hundred years ago, a philosopher named Democritus suggested that matter is made of tiny particles he called *atomos*, but most people at that time didn't agree with him. Later in the 19th century, John Dalton discovered the atomic theory, which suggested that atoms are the smallest particle and can't be subdivided. In the present time, an American theoretical physicist, Machio Kaku, explained in the documentary *The Universe in a Nutshell* that physicists deconstruct and reconstruct thousands of subatomic particles through the Standard Model of elementary particles. This model is used by physicists to understand subatomic particles and how they function. Billions of dollars and 20 Nobel prizes have gone into the design and creation of this model. One elementary particle was missing called the Higgs boson. Peter Higgs suggested the existence of this elementary particle in 1964, and its existence was confirmed in an experiment in 2012 in Geneva Switzerland, which cost upwards of $13.25 billion. According to Wikipedia, the world's biggest scientific machine, which is called the Large Hadron Collider, was built by an organization in Europe for nuclear research. This was done in collaboration with 10,000 scientists, hundreds of universities and laboratories, along with more than a hundred countries in order to confirm the existence of the Higgs boson elementary particle. Machio Kaku further stated that the next particles to be discovered in the future are called sparticles or super particles. The beauty of infinity exists in space and inside matter as well.

Allah, our Creator, is extremely powerful and super intelligent and is the only source of strength to save us from pain and show us the right path to true success and happiness. We should strengthen our relationship with Him and remember our Creator every day and show our gratitude for such limitless blessings. We should observe and think about the beauty created by Allah. There are a lot of attractions around us. Things are not only beautiful, but they have multiple functions, too. For example, a rose looks so beautiful and smells nice, and its beauty attracts bees, which causes cross-pollination. Bees make honey from it, and we get scents from it. We also use it as an expression of love to give to our loved ones as a gift.

Another beautiful thing I want to mention is water. Do you ever think about how beautiful water is and how many functions it has? We drink water to satisfy our thirst. We bathe with it. We wash with it. It helps in regulating temperature, whether it's our car or our environment. It helps to grow crops, provides us with seafood and allows ships to travel across the world for business and pleasure. Water is life and extremely important to us. We can survive for days on water alone. Think about the system that distributes water around the world. The sun evaporates water from oceans. These vapors make beautiful clouds, and these clouds travel the globe then descend in the form of rain and snow. The snow melts because of the heat from the sun and seeps water into the ground, and we can build wells or boreholes to extract this accumulated water. We can then purify and drink it. The cycle goes on and on.

The purpose of this chapter is to encourage you to look around, see the beauty everywhere, think, and meditate. You will see lots of instances of intelligence even in tiny insects, like the ant, which has the ability to survive no matter how many years have passed, how they collect food, reproduce, and survive, and how intelligent these tiny creatures are. Appreciating nature and thinking about how it impacts us is essential because we can thank our Creator for these blessings. I leave you with this. Take a short stroll in your local park and observe the nature around you. Don't carry any headphones and listen. By paying attention and listening closely, our environment comes alive. Take a few deep breaths, and when you exhale, smile. I assure you that you will feel invigorated. Take a moment to appreciate this because our Creator took a moment to create it. The moment you acknowledge and live in the present, your relationship with our Creator will be stronger and joyous. As the saying and children's rhyme goes, "Count your blessings, one by one."

Chapter 10

THE SPONTANEOUS COMPLEX

I heard a story not long ago about a young girl who asked Sadhguru if he ever got a superiority complex. As an Indian yogi and author, Sadhguru replied by saying, "The question is not about superiority complex, inferiority complex, poverty complex or wealthy complex; it should be that there's a necessity to have a complex. This is a serious problem, whatever kind it is. By having a complex, you have assumed something about yourself, and you have concretized that assumption in such a way, you believe everything that is associated with it. You refuse to be openminded about differing opinions, and in most cases, make a bloody fool of yourself wherever you go." I agree with Sadhguru on this. Having a complex, which inflates one's ego, has caused wars, arguments, and death. Individuals, who choose to be stuck in their ways, refusing to be empathetic to other people's plights, have been the source of the deteriorating human condition. But because we are inherently flawed, we fall into a pattern, oscillating between different complexes in our lifetimes.

My observation is that almost every human being is living with both superiority and inferiority complexes simultaneously. The mood is switched spontaneously between the two at times. For example, in a hospital, if a ward boy meets with a cleaner, the mood of the ward boy shifts to superiority. If the same ward boy meets with a nurse, the nurse's mood shifts to superiority, and the ward boy's mood shifts to inferiority. If a nurse meets with a medical officer (doctor), the mood of the nurse changes spontaneously, and if the medical officer meets with a consultant, his mood and behavior changes, too. I'm sure you get the gist. We live in a spontaneous complex that changes according to the situations or the people we meet. You might have heard of the term, spontaneous complex, for the first time because this is a term of my creation, and what I mean is that it is a complex, which switches from one to the other automatically, and we aren't aware of its shifts. If we are not mindful of it, we cannot control it, but it happens to us every day. Like spontaneous breathing, it happens. Most of the time, we are not aware of our breathing, but we breathe because it is spontaneous. Now you have an idea what I mean by spontaneous complex.

As I've mentioned, Sadhguru believed that any kind of complex is a serious problem, and, in my opinion, more than 90 percent of people live in a spontaneous complex, so more than 90 percent of people have a severe problem. You could deduce that this spontaneous complex can limit one's potential. However, the good news is that we can break from this pattern, allowing us to clear our minds and connect us to reality. We can apply some effective strategies that will break the superficial or illusionist assumptions. Most people fall in this trap out of fear of being fired for speaking up or being insubordinate. They fear the consequences of presenting oneself as a threat to the other person's complex and ego. They fear standing out like a sore thumb because usually people who do so end up as a target. Just because someone is your boss or is older than you doesn't mean you have to lower your potential to appease them. You can still be respectful and at the same time assertive.

We can break the pattern of our spontaneous complex and see reality only when we realize our true value and judge ourselves and other people as valuable beings rather than making assumptions on external appearance. Everyone has equal value, and as we estimated in the third chapter, the value of being alive is 95 quadrillion dollars or, said differently, 95 thousand trillion dollars. Every human is equally valuable, and when you realize that, your spontaneous complex will be nipped in the bud. So, whenever you meet other people from different walks of life, whether it is a cleaner or doctor, you will see them as precious beings. Some professions deserve a little more respect because of their impact on improving the human condition. People who are doctors, scientists, and teachers take years to learn how to improve our quality of life, so they receive a little more respect in society. You will get this concept more clearly after the following example.

This analogy follows an individual who has three big precious blue diamonds. Each diamond has the same price, 20 million dollars, in the market. He puts one diamond in a beautiful pouch made of costly silk, the second in another pouch made of white gold material, and the third in a pouch made of dirty cheap cloth. Which diamond is worth more? Does the material of the pouch determine their worth? Or do all diamonds have the same value? All the diamonds are the same except for the different materials of the pouches. The pouches may add a few hundred dollars to their value, which is negligible as compared to 20 million dollars. They only add it based on external appearance, but this value is short-lived once the diamonds are removed from them. Then they just become pieces of material.

Every human has more value than a diamond, which is limitless, and it doesn't matter if someone puts on cheap or expensive clothing, lives in a small or an expensive house, or has a cheap or an exotic car. All humans have infinite value. Their external differences are negligible as compared to their true value as human beings. The most valuable thing is life and being human. If we add a number, big or small, to infinite value, the sum will be infinite, so we are all equal. There is no point of living with a complex because we are all the same. That's why Sadhguru called them fools because their mind judges others based on superficial appearance and misses out on the diamond within. All humans are extremely valuable that's why I called them diamonds. Now, it's up to you to judge the diamond or the pouch. If you judge an individual based on their inner worth or the diamond within, you will see their infinite value and break free from the spontaneous complex pattern. However, if you judge the pouch or the external appearance, you will definitely remain stuck in this loop.

I explained the same concept to one of my friends after he told me about his complex, and he was listening to me attentively. After a few days, he approached and thanked me. The concept helped him see others as precious rather than judging them on their external appearance. My friend broke out of his spontaneous complex, which helped him to see the reality. One day, he told me that a new staff nurse had joined them, who was not good looking. Other colleagues judged her as being unattractive and did not talk to her, but my friend said, "She is a diamond." My friend did not judge her value on external looks, but he was aware of her value as a human being. After he broke free from his spontaneous complex mood, he saw every human as a diamond. He judged them on their true infinite value.

To conclude this chapter, we have infinite value and the external appearances or the possession of materialistic things add little to it, which is negligible as compared to the true value of life. The reality many times could be that some individuals put on a façade and make you think their outer appearance matches their inner worth. You may see a beggar on the street and think that they have no value in society. You've judged them based on their present circumstance. What you may not know is that the beggar is an army vet with undiagnosed PTSD, or it could be the opposite. You see a woman driving the latest BMW, wearing the latest designer shoes, and carrying a Gucci handbag. What you don't know is that she is headed to court because of stealing millions from pensioners. The realization of this insight will free us from the spontaneous complex pattern mood and connect us to reality, which gives us the best experiences and improves our relations with others.

Chapter 11

HOW TO DEAL WITH ASSHOLES.

Have you ever been near someone who drains your energy? Their negativity seeps through everything and anything they touch. They occupy your thoughts because of their presence. Whenever I went to school or to my work place, there seemed to be an abundance of assholes around me. Some assholes tease people intentionally, and others do it unintentionally and cause lots of tension and stress. Some are analytical and target specific people who they think will have an inferiority complex and will not fight back. I'm sure you've heard of the personality types: narcissist and sociopath. These personality types are usually smart individuals who know what to do and say to come off as genuine but somehow leave you feeling unworthy. They are wolves in sheep's clothing and believe in their own superiority. These personality types can form from early in life, especially if something drastic happened during one of the psychosocial stages. A rift occurs between their sense of morality and reality, and for them, the universe revolves around them. These assholes tend to infiltrate and ruin a peaceful existence without much effort from their part. They are skilled manipulators, and I have become wary of coming across one of them.

Then I learnt something positive, which changed my assumption about these people. We humans are important to each other and to the system as a whole. Let me explain how we are important to each other even if we do not like each other and, to some extent, want to avoid getting trapped into a web of lies. If you imagine the world is like one system, like one body, and every individual is like a single cell of this body, you arrive at the conclusion that this world has billions of cells formed from humans. If we hate each other and damage each other, we are damaging the whole system. As we know, our body has billions of cells. These cells make different organs, and different organs perform different functions to make one whole system. All organs support each other and coordinate to make the system work effectively, like the heart pumps blood to the entire body to perfuse cells, kidneys filter blood and keep it clean and excrete waste in the form of urine, and our immune system is always active to detect and destroy unfriendly organisms and maintain our body. But what if the organs stop coordinating and start attacking each other? For example, what happens if the heart doesn't like the kidney and refuses to perfuse them? What happens if the heart puts a sanction on the kidneys and reduces blood supply to them? The kidneys will stop filtering blood in response, and the whole body will soon be full of waste. The system will soon fail to work, and body will get sick and die. Until the heart and kidney restore coordination, the system will not work efficiently.

Our human story is similar because we are the cells of the world. If we start to hate each other, we are sickening the world. Living in a sick world is not beneficial because the sick world causes huge disasters, and who suffers? We do. It has happened time and time again when countries with leaders, who have a superiority complex, have gone to war. Many times, these wars begin as a way of showing off who has the most expensive weaponry. These leaders make decisions behind protected walls with repercussions never reaching them. If we could have avoided all historical wars, the world might have been a better place. Climate change is another critical issue and has become a man-made problem. We forget that we need this planet to stay alive, and we need each other to maintain our existence. So, we need to be 'one race, one people,' and promote love and help each other to increase the pace of development. It may be challenging to forgive narcissists and sociopaths, but we need to understand that these people need medical intervention to become better.

The heart is a symbol of love, and when we love someone, we relate them to the heart. We cannot live without the heart, so it's a vital organ for us. Our loved ones are equally as important to us. We need each other to survive. On the contrary, when we hate someone, we call them an asshole because the asshole, as a part of our body, performs an essential but dirty function. Can we survive without an asshole? The answer is no because we excrete waste through them, so it is as important to us as the heart is. In the same way that those people we love are important, those we label as assholes are also important for the whole system to function effectively. Once we realize that we need each other, we will all detract from trying to outdo each other and build on our lives.

We are reactive beings, so our behavior will be reflected back to us. The saying, "Treat others the way you want to be treated," is essential here. You can think of our engagement with one another as transactions. When you buy groceries, you expect that the value of money you pay will equate to the products you need. When the prices rise, say a liter of milk rising from 5 dollars to 20 dollars overnight, this hike in price will anger you. You will feel shortchanged and will demand to know why the price has increased that much. Similarly, when your behavior is hostile towards someone else, you can't expect or demand them to be nice to you. That's not how it works. In some cases, they are conscious people who do not react in this manner, and whether you are nice or rude to them, they will be kind. But these people are few and far between. We are inherently reactionary.

In my life, I have come across a few assholes and one such situation changed the course of my life. A bonafide bully enjoyed teasing me. Not only me but everyone had been teased and bullied by him in our hostel. I tried to be nice to him, but he would not stop. In fact, I think my behavior towards him egged him on. One day, we exchanged a few harsh words, and after that, I stopped talking to him even though he tried to talk to me. I utterly ignored him because I thought at that time it was the only way to live my life peacefully. A few months later, I learnt his father had had a heart attack, so he had to go home to be with the rest of the family. I knew he was short on money, so I visited him in his room. After a few brief moments, I offered him some money to help him out. He did not take the money from me, but after that, his behavior changed. He began to respect my boundaries. I think his behavior changed because I showed I cared and provided support during his hard times. I understood that sometimes people are hostile as a defense mechanism—that they might have been hurt by people before, so they are rude and obnoxious to keep people at arm's length. The saying, "*Hurt* people, hurt *people*," is appropriate here. Though it is unacceptable behavior, understanding why people behave the way they do will dampen your own reactionary behavior as theirs may be a subconscious move. Our harsh reactions may exacerbate situations without knowing.

We should be more concerned about our reactionary behavior rather than reacting to assholes, whether subconsciously or unconsciously, in other words, developing an awareness of our thought patterns and emotions. To become less reactionary, we should improve our consciousness or awareness about our thought patterns, emotions, and behavior. Once we become aware of these, we have control over everything about ourselves. How can we control it or change it if we are not aware of it? The greater awareness we have, the more we can control our behavior. To improve our conscious level, we have to adopt some interventions, like meditation and reading books that can expand our understanding about ourselves and others.

I would like to share a few tips and insights from a bestseller spiritual book. One of my favorite books is *The Four Agreements* by Don Miguel Ruiz. "Be impeccable with your word" is the first lesson, and what Ruiz calls an agreement. In this agreement, we should understand that our words have a great impact on others. If we use positive words, things will run like a well-oiled machine, but if we use negative words, situations may turn sour. Having a positive behavior radiates confidence and inclusivity. You become approachable, and though assholes may see you as a target, they will soon tire of targeting you because they realize you are genuinely being yourself. The more we use positive words in our language and behavior, the fewer assholes will be around you. The second agreement is that we "don't take anything personally." If someone tells you that you are stupid and you agree and accept their words as truth, it's like accepting to be willingly poisoned. Most people are so obsessed with themselves and are always thinking about how they can take advantage of others for their benefit so that's why they always take things personally.

If your boss is angry at you or someone says something rude, you should not take it personally because they may be having a bad day or are having issues in their personal lives. We don't know all the facts. We can't see the bigger picture. The third agreement is that we "don't make assumptions." Sometimes without any proof or facts, we assume that individual's actions without thinking about other aspects. If we don't step back from those situations, we may make things worse. The asshole is not a problem, but how we perceive things and respond to them is. Instead of judging other people, we should be aware of our perceptions and patterns of thought and should train our mind to see the positive side of things rather than the opposite.

To summarize, everyone plays a vital role in ensuring the system works. If we place a negative label on some individuals, especially those who are acting contrary to society's expectations, our subconscious behavior and reactions will reveal that we do not like them, which will enhance their reactivity further. These individuals will continue to feed off that negativity and reinforce their behavior, thinking that they might as well continue acting like assholes because everyone thinks they are. We should accept them as they are and help them realize their true worth. They don't have to try and outdo another to get what they want in life. They can still be the boss and a winner without being an asshole. We should take steps to enhance our awareness to break free from these unconscious thought patterns.

Chapter 12

HOW CHRONIC STRESS
AFFECTS OUR HEALTH

To understand the effects of chronic stress on our health, we need to understand the General Adaptation theory by Han Selye, a pioneering Hungarian-Canadian endocrinologist and researcher, who is considered the father of stress. Not that he is the first person to get stressed, but he came up with the theory of general adaptation syndrome or GAS, a three-stage process that describes the physiological changes the body goes through when under stress. The stages are (a) alarming stage, (b) resistance stage, and (c) exhaustion stage.

When a person is exposed to a dangerous or demanding situation, whether it's physiological or psychological, the first stage, or the fight and flight response, is activated. In this stage, the body produces sympathetic activity, which produces stress hormones and boosts adrenaline. This causes the following symptoms: high blood pressure, increased blood glucose level, dilated pupils and more blood flow to muscles. This makes some systems slow down, like reducing activity to our immune system and gastrointestinal system. The alarming stage is good for us, and it gives us more energy and saves us in dangerous situations. When the alarming stage is over, the body has to rest, so it activates the parasympathetic system, which inhibits activated stress hormones. This allows our blood pressure to return to normal and reactivates our gastrointestinal system and immune system, giving energy to our cells. This helps heal any small damages or wears and tears at the cellular level that may have occurred.

In the second stage, or the resistance stage, the stressor exists for an extended period of time, like if someone is jobless, has been diagnosed with a disease, or is dealing with other real or perceived life situations. A lengthy, stress response causes hormones that are usually helpful in the short-term to remain active for a longer time. This causes damage to different organs. Every day, small wears and tears occur in the body, and they do not heal because the continuous stress has deactivated the immune system. These wears and tears accumulate with a passage of time, and in this stage, the body can resist the stress response. However, our body cannot maintain resistance for a very long time. At this point, the person experiences irritability, frustration, and poor concentration. If the stress continues and the body utilizes all its resources, it will lead the person to the third stage, which is exhaustion phase. Exhaustion stage is the third and last phase in which all the energy is drained and the body has utilized all its resources. The individual becomes depressed, burnt out, and develops stress-related diseases, such as hypertension, diabetes, obesity, and depression.

Selye's theory succinctly describes what happens to our bodies when we are stressed: our health deteriorates, and our productivity lowers. Nowadays, there's a lot to be stressed about. Just recently, the world faced a global crisis—COVID-19. We were on lockdown. Some of us lost our jobs, and others had to remain home for long periods of time. Some of us lost loved ones to this crisis. Many people are still suffering, and if they do not find positive coping strategies, they are more prone to developing depression and other diseases. To be healthy in the long run, we should avoid chronic stress, and we should keep ourselves relaxed, have better sleep patterns, and increase our chances of remaining alive. Our immune system activates when we are relaxed, so meditation, breathing exercises, better sleep, and other stress-relieving practices can boost our immune system and keep us healthy.

SECTION II

RANDOM POSITIVE THOUGHTS

Chapter 13

WRITING

I learnt the importance of this technique from a spiritual teacher—to write down thoughts, especially when something happens that has disturbed your daily activity or sleep. After learning this technique, whenever my mind was full of thoughts, and I felt heavy and disturbed, I wrote them down, and afterwards, I felt so light immediately. I felt like a burden had been lifted from my shoulders, as if I had discovered a cure for insanity. As time passed, I also started writing down positive thoughts, which helped me cope with life. This section of the book is a collection of positive thoughts that have had an impact on my life. These positive thoughts come to mind randomly, so that's why I call them random positive thoughts. The chapters in this section are short and may or may not connect with each other, but every chapter has something to help you in your life.

Writing is a very positive activity and can allow us to connect with ourselves. It can be therapeutic, too. We are blessed with conscious and subconscious faculties. With the passage of time, our experiences are stored in our subconscious, and they become part of us and produce patterns of thoughts in our mind. This affects our behavior and moods, and that's why mood swings happen. Sometimes we feel depressed, and other times, we feel blessed. Writing these thoughts makes us more conscious and aware. When we are aware of these thoughts, we can control them and act appropriately. Otherwise, these thoughts or our subconscious mind will control our moods and our behaviors. When you take up writing as a hobby, it will bring more awareness to your subconscious mind. So, write whenever you feel that your mind is full of thoughts or whenever you are feeling depressed, irritated, and aggressive. Just write and don't worry about the structure of what you're writing. You should write what comes to your mind and forget about grammar or sentence structure or spelling mistakes because it's only for you. You are not publishing it. It will help you to be aware of your mind and emotions and will bring more calmness and clarity to your life. I task you with this. Find a piece of paper and pen and answer this question: "What am I most grateful for today?"

Chapter 14

A GLASS HALF FULL
IS A BETTER PERSPECTIVE

T he following two paragraphs are in italics, and I wrote them when I was going through a rough patch. By writing down my thoughts, I became aware and conscious of my mind and the thoughts oscillating within it. You will have an idea after reading the reason I extracted these two paragraphs from my diary and included them in this book.

"Today, I developed an insight that I still have a lot of time to live. I am 30 years old, and our country's total life span for a male is 65 years, so if I don't get into an accident, I can live for an additional 35 years. I can live longer by adopting a healthy lifestyle. I have a lot of time. So, I have to create new habits to achieve my goals, like studying—acquiring knowledge to increase my career prospects and improving my position and salary. I can exercise and adopt a balanced diet. I can improve my health and have a six-pack. By reading good books, I can enhance my

knowledge, make better decisions, and improve my quality of life.

The first thing I need to figure out is what I want to do in the next 35 years. The decision is up to me. Do I want to go on a world tour or make more money? Or develop a nice body? Or learn martial arts? Or learn new languages? Or learn how to write? Or learn about my religion? There's a lot I can do. The world is my oyster. Time should not be wasted and should be spent on what I like to do instead of being depressed and crying. The more things I want to learn, the more time and energy it requires. The proverb, "Jackal of everything is the master of nothing," pops into mind. I understand I should choose a few things that I want to achieve in the next 35 years. One step at a time. For now, my priority is to improve my career prospects by developing my skills and adding to my knowledge bank."

The above thoughts are good examples of looking at the glass half full. I wrote these thoughts in my diary when I was having bad days, and because of these positive thoughts, I found a better job as a lecturer in a nursing college and increased my salary four-fold as compared to my previous salary. I am also working on this book. In five years, I have improved my quality of life by remaining positive and working on things. To see the glass half full is a better perspective. It brings a positive attitude with positive energy, and you will be unstoppable.

You can try this, too. Calculate the life expectancy in your country and subtract your current age. Use your remaining time wisely instead of being depressed and crying over spilt milk. Get a pen and paper and write down what you'd really like to do or want to achieve. Make goals and read books (or use any other medium that you are interested in) on how to make smart decisions and the different ways you can achieve them. You can learn from other great minds. A wise man once said, "When the student is ready, the teacher will appear." Whatever you want to learn, you can, because you have the ability to learn. Pursue your goals every day, test your potential at optimum level, and set an example for others. Always count your blessings, never focus on what you are lacking, rather than what you already have, and build on that. I'd like to conclude with this beautiful quote by Eddie Money, "To me, the glass is always half full, never half empty."

Chapter 15

SLEEP

The better you sleep, the better your performance will be the next day. Sleep recharges your battery and heals the body, so the next day, you will feel fresh, creative, and more productive. Quality of sleep also improves memory, reduces stress, and reduces the risk of depression and cancer. After a stressful day, our addictive mind works nonstop. Anxious and negative thoughts usually permeate us, which can drain our energy and cause us to be frustrated and irritable, so sleep is the best way to stop your mind from producing negative and anxious thoughts. If you are facing an issue in your life and notice those thoughts drain your energy, you should sleep on it. Wake up the next day with a fresh mind and a renewed perspective, which will allow you to produce a better solution for that issue. When we are asleep, our body heals, so at least you will save your body from further damage from the stress.

Quality sleep directly affects our health and our productivity. Reading about what methods ensure quality sleep and what activities and food helps us to fall asleep easier will allow you to develop useful strategies that are tailored for you. Sleep is the best medicine and is a blessing. I realized this when I used to work 12-hour night shift duties. During night duties, I thought those who were sleeping in their home were fortunate people, but a lot of people do not realize this blessing. They stay awake late at night with their thoughts dipped in negativity. Remember, a healthy mind is a healthy life. Quality sleep is essential for our health and better productivity, so we need to intervene to improve on it.

Chapter 16

SETTLE DOWN
LIKE WATER

Sometimes we become tired of having persistent negative thoughts revolving around what is happening in our lives or when someone does something wrong to us. Try as we might, we try to sleep, but our minds keep us awake. The human mind has some tendencies, getting stuck in the past or planning for the future, and it needs to be in control of everything and anything. These tendencies are unhealthy and being a control freak is not a good strategy. Osho once said that he prefers to float than swim. Controlling everything is like swimming against the river tide. Swimming against the river is an analogy which implies that there are lots of things in the world beyond our control. If we do not stop trying to control everything, we will be exhausted, and our energy completely drained. We will not have the motivation to do the things we like because the negativity has zapped all our energy. This can have negative effects on our health, relationships, and career.

Sometimes going to sleep or taking a nap helps alleviate our mood. One day, I was trying hard to sleep but failed to do so. I sat down because I was thirsty. There was a bottle of water beside me, so I drank some water and put it back. I observed the water inside the transparent bottle and noticed that the water was disturbed as I put it back, but slowly it settled down by itself. I shook the bottle again and did this action many times. Based on my observations, the water doesn't force itself to settle down, but it takes its time. At that moment, a lovely quote by Bruce Lee came to mind that says, "Empty your mind. Be formless, shapeless, like water. You put water into a bottle, it becomes the bottle, you put water into a teapot, it becomes the teapot. Water can flow, or it can crash. Be water, my friend." So, I was thinking about how I can be like water. I remembered that we are already water because our body is almost 70 percent water, so that means we can mimic its behavior and rest our bodies in the same way. I lay in my bed and tried to settle my thoughts. I stopped forcing myself to fall asleep and let my mind relax by itself, and in no time, I slept. That day, I learned an exceptional lesson from water: when water was disturbed, it settled down by itself, and even though I repeatedly shook it, the water took its own time to settle.

The moral of the story is, we are similar to water because our life situations may cause us to be distressed and rowdy. But just like water, we should give our minds time to absorb and adapt to our life situation. We should relinquish control over the things we don't have the power to monitor. Worrying doesn't help. Sleep will come easily if we settle our thoughts like water. So, "Be water, my friend."

Chapter 17

GETTING RID OF ADDICTION

Most humans may have an addiction in their lives. Addiction is the frequent and chronic use of substances or activities which can harm us physically, mentally, and socially. It directly affects our health, relationships, and productivity, and we are unable to quit even if we want to. According to brainz.org, the top ten common addictions are related to "alcohol, smoking or tobacco, gambling, food, videos games, internet, sex, shopping and work." There are different causes or risk factors associated with addiction, including genetic, poor support system, trauma, younger age, or some kind of mental health issue. There is one thing common in any addiction, and it is that they give us pleasure, thus causing an increase of neurotransmitters (dopamine) and act on our reward system.

We get pleasure from addiction for a short time, but in the long run, it damages our health, relationships, and productivity. The good news for those who want to quit an addiction is it is treatable. Some addicts need professional help while others can treat it themselves. The first step to quitting an addiction is to realize you have a problem. If you believe it's good for you, then it's impossible to quit. Acknowledging that the short-lived pleasurable effects are harmful to your body requires an awareness of the chemical effects within your body. You should also think about the financial ramifications of maintaining your addictive habit. Think about how much money you will save once you quit. You can finally take that holiday you have always wanted. The second step is to make a goal to overcome any hurdles that may come your way. For example, if you are a smoker, then your goal is to quit smoking, or if you are addicted to watching porn, your goal is to quit watching porn. The third step is to make an objective. The difference between a goal and an objective is the latter is quantitative, which can be measured. By reducing the quantity, you can wean yourself off the addiction. For example, for a smoker who smokes on average 20 cigarettes a day, the best objective for them is to reduce to 15 cigarettes in a day for one month, and the second objective is to spend 30 minutes reading an article or watching a TED talk related to the effects of smoking and how one can quit it. By replacing a bad habit with a positive one, an individual can begin to trick their mind and reduce the quantity of their addiction. Soon, they'll pick up the habit of reading positive self-help books and have no need for the short-term pleasures of an addiction.

The technique, which I recommend because it really works, is tapering down things slowly. Taper down or taper up is a technique used by doctors or nurses who introduce prescribed drugs to achieve desired effects in different medical conditions. Tapering down is the best strategy because if we suddenly stop using a drug, the body cannot manage because it is adapted to that drug, so we taper down slowly to allow the body to adjust to it. It's important to note that quitting is not easy, and sometimes going cold turkey can make it easy for you to relapse.

I know a friend, my best friend, who used to smoke 20 cigarettes a day and wanted to quit. He had committed to quitting several times but to no avail. On one occasion, there was a no smoking day at our college, and he made a commitment to quit on that day. However, after a week, he was back to smoking again. The problem with quitting is that the body is used to that substance, so the sudden drop in the quantity of the substance led to severe withdrawal effects. These effects are what cause an individual to relapse. They start to wallow in the fact that they are in pain, and the only way to stop being in pain is to take the substance. They think that they can't live without it and that life will be better off if consumption is continued. But that's what addiction is. It tricks your body into thinking that you cannot survive without it. You begin to miss the euphoria and wish to experience it one more time. Even though you have made a commitment, you yearn to feel that level of calmness and pleasure, so that's why I use the term taper down instead of quitting because it is an achievable and measurable objective. It is based on strategies instead of emotions, and if a person does taper down, they gain one step closer to their goal. This progress will produce some positive emotions, which will motivate them further. The body will easily adjust to the change, and if we taper down a substance, there will be no or feeble withdrawal effects.

My friend tapered down his smoking from 20 cigarettes to 0 per day, and now he smokes very rarely—once or twice in the whole year—whenever he meets with his old friends. Smoking one cigarette after six months did not break his commitment because he has no commitment to quit, but he is happy because he tapered it down from 20 cigarettes per day to one or two cigarettes in a year. Smoking one or two cigarettes in a year is not an addiction because he is not dependent on it. He doesn't obsess over it. He can go for months without needing to smoke. At the beginning of this process, my friend observed the behaviors and situations that stimulated him to smoke. He analyzed that there were a few triggers that caused him to smoke. These triggers were linked to stressful situations and a habitual after-lunch smoke. He also noticed there are some situations in which he could easily ignore the stimulus by being aware of his thoughts. If he was around another friend who was a smoker, and they lit a cigarette, this would trigger his stimulus to light one as well. But this stimulus was not strong enough and could be easily ignored.

After a few days of observation, he analyzed that there were five to seven cigarettes that he smoked unnecessarily and could be avoided, so he made an objective for the month that he would smoke only 15 cigarettes in a day. The next month, he made a new objective that he would buy the small packet, which had 10 cigarettes because the fewer cigarettes he had, the fewer he would smoke. He would also only smoke when there was a powerful stimulus that he couldn't ignore. The next month, he developed a new strategy that he was not going to buy a packet of cigarettes. When the stimulus was strong enough, he would have to go to the market to buy one cigarette. This was how he could ignore many weak stimuli because it was inconvenient for him to go to the market and smoke. This strategy worked during the day, but at night, things were different. Late at night, he would develop strong urges to smoke, which was hard to ignore and caused some withdrawal effects, so then he used to buy only three cigarettes for the night. Long story short, after one year, he tapered down his smoking from 20 cigarettes per day to –three to five per day. I asked him why he hasn't yet quit. He stated that when he comes back from work and gets close to the shop where he used to buy cigarettes, he is drawn to it to buy cigarettes and was aware of it, but he could not ignore it.

He almost dissolved all past habitual conditions, which were associated with smoking, but few are still intact like buying cigarettes from that shop. He was happy because he tapered down smoking from 20 to three cigarettes per day. Then luckily, we both found a new job in a new city. We both worked shifts there, and on the first day, when he saw a shop, his mind gave him a command to buy some cigarettes. But his awareness allowed him to ignore this command and to continue walking past the shop. He did not want to create new conditions that would make him relapse. The new city and job provided a chance for him to smoke zero cigarettes in a day. He ignored his mind's and body's response to buying cigarettes. It took him a few years to develop this process, but he finally achieved his objectives and goals. The addiction no longer controlled him.

Our mind is a great tool if used wisely. The mind gives importance to the activities which we frequently do and reminds us again and again. The more frequent we do an activity, the more our mind gives importance to it and reminds us. In contrast, the more we ignore an activity, the less importance our mind makes it and does not remind us. So, giving importance to an activity according to its frequency, is an untapped code. It means that if you want your mind to give importance to a specific task, you should do that task frequently, and if you want your mind forget about a specific task, you should stop doing it. If you want your mind to give importance to an activity, you should perform it frequently instead of trying to convince your mind by reasoning and rationalizing things. So, this is how my friend's mind stopped producing the command to smoke because he tapered down that activity and stopped it completely in the right circumstance.

In conclusion, if someone wants to overcome their addiction, the best way is to taper it down and find a suitable living arrangement that will minimize your impulses and triggers associated with your addictive behavior. The key is to taper it down to the point when it is easy to avoid and look for the right circumstances which can help you to avoid it completely. Tapering down is a better strategy than committing to quit suddenly. It is also important to note the role of peer influence as a major contributor to persistent addiction. If you want to taper down your substance use, you need to surround yourself with people who are non-addicts. By continuously hanging around people who are addicted to the same substance as you, your mind continues to normalize this behavior, and you start to see it as the new norm. This may mean that you lose a few friends, but at least you will be living a healthy life.

Chapter 18

FORGIVENESS

"When you hold onto resentment towards another, you are bound to that person or condition by an emotional link that is stronger than steel. Forgiveness is the only way to dissolve that link and get free."

— *Katherine Ponder.*

We know everything needs energy to function, whether it's a car, a mobile phone, a singing baby doll, our body, our mind, or our immune system. If there is no energy or a lack of energy, it directly affects its functions. Resentment, guilt, blame, or any other negative thoughts are the energy vampire. When we are triggered by something, negativity sucks and drains our energy, spoiling our mood and causing further problems. These energy vampires are like virus programs, which drain our battery and make our operating system (our mind) slower and less effective.

Our body has a finite amount of energy and resources at its disposal. If these negative thoughts persist for a long time, our limited energy resources are depleted, and our body is no longer able to heal itself. These negative thought patterns can cause different diseases, like diabetic mellitus, cardiovascular diseases, and cancer. If your negative thoughts are activated because someone did something bad to you, and now you are consumed with revenge, you will be distressed. Your mind and body will remain active, planning out how you will cause harm to the other person. These negative thoughts will take over your life, and you will start to think that the only way to regain a peaceful existence is by retaliating. Distress is chronic stress in which our body is unable to heal from the wears and tears that happen to our body on a daily basis. Distress keeps sympathetic response activated, which deactivates our immune system, so if it continues for a long time and if we remain in this persistent stage of stress, our immune system will not function properly, and we can end up catching diseases that cause tumors (cancer).

Since I was a young child, I had been hearing that forgiveness is the best policy, but I didn't understand it until recently. It's the best strategy to stop draining our vital energy. We need this energy to achieve constructive goals, which can give us more benefits and make us happy instead of wasting it on taking revenge and wallowing in destructive negative thoughts or activities. That is why all spiritual teachers are big fans of forgiveness, and there is no second opinion that forgiveness is not good for us. The first person to be forgiven is your own self. Everyone has a lot of guilt because we are humans, and to err is human. We are inherently flawed and make mistakes. Our Creator designed us in such a way that when we make mistakes, we can choose to learn from them. Angels do not make mistakes because they have been designed that way. We are not angels. We are humans, and if we do not forgive ourselves, how can we make progress in our lives? A mind that is stuck wallowing in negative thoughts has very low frequency, which attracts only negative situations and people. Useless and destructive thoughts make us dysfunctional and insane. When something happens, we should acknowledge it and forgive ourselves. You should give yourself credit for trying and cut yourself some slack. The universe was not created in one day, and you can't expect your true potential to come to fruition immediately. There will be a few bumps on the road, including other people who have negative intentions towards you.

After we forgive ourselves, we should forgive those who are close to us, like young people who have problems with their parents and believe their parents are responsible for their failures or their parents did something to them which has negative outcomes. Parents want the best for their children. Their intentions are always noble, but sometimes their execution is terrible. We should remember that they are humans first, then our parents. On the other hand, parents may feel the same way. If you are a parent and have a problem with your children, you may have done everything for them, but they don't appreciate it. You may believe they are not doing things for you and do not care about you, so we should forgive them. The loved ones who we want to forgive after ourselves are parents, children, spouses, siblings, and best friends. Third, we should forgive everyone else—whoever we have met since childhood. We should do a flashback, searching for those who bullied, betrayed, or hurt us from childhood up until now. Whatever they have done to you, we have to forgive them all. Why should we forgive them? It's not because they deserve it, but we should forgive them for our own sake because we should be concerned about our health and we want to make progress in life. We should forgive them because we are also humans and we can make mistakes, so sometimes we need forgiveness, too. If we can't forgive others, how can we expect forgiveness from others?

When I realized the importance of forgiveness, I choose one special night a month to look back and forgive. That night, I reminisce on my past, extract those trapped negative thoughts in my mind, forgive them all, and break free from those trapped negative thoughts. I realize this is important for my well-being. A few years ago, I met a wise and kind man who was also a big fan of forgiveness and told me one of his stories. Someone had done something bad to him, and that person had apologized later. He told that person he had already forgiven them. In other words, the nice wise man forgave him before he sought an apology. The lesson in this chapter is that forgiveness improves our quality of life and frees us from the burden of resentment. We should forgive ourselves, our loved ones, and all those who have wronged us in the past. Forgiveness stops draining our energy and boosts our immune system. I will conclude this chapter with this beautiful quote from Martin Luther King, Jr. "Darkness cannot drive out darkness; only light can do that. Hate cannot drive out hate; only love can do that."

Chapter 19

DIAPHRAGMATIC BREATHING

I had a dream one night. In the dream, I saw something trickling down from my nose. It was black in color and sticky in texture, plus it had three small screws. It looked like that black parasite which is called a leech and sucks blood. In those days, I was struggling with some addictive patterns of negative thinking. I inferred from this dream that the black sticky thing with screws symbolized addictions or negative thoughts. When it emerged through my nose, a clue about how to get rid of the negative patterns presented itself. Clinical psychologist, Megan Riehl, suggests that diaphragmatic breathing reduces stress whilst simultaneously allows for a gentle massage of the intestines and stomach. Whenever I was alone in my room and found compulsive, unwanted thoughts in my mind, I used this breathing and meditation technique to thwart these thoughts. I began by placing a hand on my chest and the other on my stomach. I inhaled and exhaled through my nose and noticed that after 15 to 30 minutes, I felt so refreshed and rejuvenated.

When we start focusing on breathing and noticing the flow of air, it stops us from thinking about other things. Our attention is placed on breathing, and the mind is no longer able to think about anything else. Here's an analogy to understand this concept. Computers and mobile phones need an internet connection to update apps and keep them active in the background, which leads to the gadgets losing power. Similarly, our mind also runs many background apps, working 24/7 to get things done. Many times, these thoughts are negative in nature and can harm us and drain our energy. The attention works like an internet connection for the mind. If we disconnect from it and focus on our breathing, all other active background apps will start being deactivated, just like when we disconnect from the internet and all background apps stop working. This is how we can stop compulsive negative thinking, but it is difficult because our mind is very intelligent. It tricks us again, hijacks our attention, and starts thinking about our problems. So, we have to play the tug of war game with our mind, and in this game, whoever pulls the attention will win. If you pull the attention and place it on other useful activities like breathing, you win, but if your mind pulls the attention back, your mind wins and takes control. We can pull the attention from our mind for at least 15 to 30 minutes and place it on diaphragmatic breathing before we go to bed or whenever we want to make ourselves feel relaxed. It's a practical meditation technique, and it doesn't need a special posture or environment.

Addictive behavior is dependent on addictive thinking. The more we repeat an activity, the more control it has because of neuroplasticity. Our brain has the ability to change and strengthen or weaken the synapses (connections) between neurons over time, and this depends on the repetition of an activity. The more we repeat a behavior, the more that synapses strengthen, and if we avoid a behavior, the synapses between neurons loosen and weaken. This is when addictive thoughts or activities inhibit a positive outlook on life. In other worlds, focusing on breathing stops addictive thinking and creates space in those thoughts. If we repeat this process again and again, the synapses, which are responsible for addictive thinking will loosen, and we can get rid of those addictive thoughts, which drain our energy and make us stressed and less productive.

It is simple. Whenever you want to inhibit neurons, which are responses for addictive thoughts patterns, you just have to focus on breathing through your nostrils. When you start focusing your breathing in this way, new types of neurons will be activated through neuroplasticity, which will allow you to break free from those unwanted thought patterns. If you divert your attention to focus in this way, it will cease all addictive behavior. Quitting a bad habit requires discipline. If you practice this technique repeatedly, it will also enhance the power you have over your mind because all the background apps will shut down, and your mind will connect with higher intelligence, which will make you more creative and calm and will also increase awareness in the present moment. Breathing happens in the now (present moment) When you focus on breathing, you focus on the now, then you will break through from your limited self (ego or conditioned thoughts) and connect to infinite intelligence (being). This meditation will make you relax and boost your immune system by activating parasympathetic responses. It's the easiest and most effective meditation technique that you can use to protect your health. By inhibiting our negative thoughts, we can reduce our stress level. We need to boost our immune system to prevent diseases and develop a strong immune system, especially in the COVID-19 pandemic.

In the End, diaphragmatic breathing is an essential meditation tool which will allow you to break free from negative thinking. By focusing on breathing through your nose, you can restore your energy and develop a positive outlook on life. This has numerous health advantages as it activates your parasympathetic response and aids in ailments, such as abdominal pain, bloating, and constipation.

Chapter 20

DON'T TRY TOO HARD TO UNDERSTAND

Sometimes we try hard to understand things, but our mind or our understanding is not developed enough to do so. The strategy discussed in this chapter is crucial to your attempt at trying to understand things. If you are wondering how we can understand things even when we do not try, think about children and how they learn their mother tongue. They don't try to understand it or the grammatical rules or memorize vocabulary, but as they grow, they learn the language. However, if a child asks a question that is beyond their comprehension, i.e., if they ask how a child comes into this world and their parents try to explain it, do you think they will understand it? No, they will probably have more questions that will only confuse them. They will learn the answer to their question by themselves as their mind matures. Our mind needs some maturation before we try to understand some deep questions or concepts. There are some concepts a mind can understand at age 10, some at 20, some at 30 or at 40, and so on.

If you are trying to comprehend things and it works for you, go for it, but if you try hard to get a concept or if you have some deep questions about life and still don't understand, then stop trying so hard. Doing so will lead to frustration and waste your energy and time. In some cases, it will take you longer Than normal but you will understand it when the time is right. This concept helped me to understand the concepts explained in the book, *The Power of Now*, by Eckhart Tolle. As Tolle suggested at the beginning of the book, do not try to understand these concepts in your mind, but you will learn it by yourself when you practice these techniques and witness its effects as time goes by. I also recommended this book to most of my friends, and they tried hard to understand it but failed to get the message and stopped reading it. This concept mostly works on questions which are related to spirituality: What is the meaning of life? What is the purpose of the universe? What is our true purpose in the world? This concept (trying not to understand) also works for students to enable them to have a better grasp of their lectures and those concepts written in their textbooks. You can test it by yourself if you are in doubt. Select a difficult concept or topic and search for it on YouTube. Look for a reputable source and find someone who explains it well. Listen attentively and be present in the moment. When the video or the lecture is finished, evaluate your understanding of the specific topic. You will have an idea that we can understand things even when we are not trying hard to do so.

The central theme of this discourse is to avoid frustration and save our energy. Patience is essential to understanding things. Many times, we need ideas and concepts to marinate in our minds for a while before we can develop them further. Suppose someone is trying to solve a jigsaw puzzle, and there are some pieces still missing. Can they solve the jigsaw puzzle? No. It doesn't matter how much time and energy they put in. They can solve it when all the pieces are found. With the passage of time, our mind gathers essential information, like finding the missing jigsaw pieces, and once we find all pieces, our mind can understand. When your mind is working on deep questions, and you cannot find the answer, try not to get frustrated but practice this concept. It might be a hard concept that you need to enhance your knowledge, but you will only be able to understand it when you stop trying to understand it. You only need to observe, listen, and be there in the present moment.

Chapter 21

USE YOUR MIND AND USE IT CONSCIOUSLY.

Nothing can give us benefits until we use it. If we have a computer and don't use it, it's useless to us. If we have a car and don't use it, it's futile. Additionally, using a tool is not enough to get full benefits from it. We need to use things consciously to increase their benefits and utility. For example, if you have an internet connection and don't use it, it will be useless to you, but if you use it and surf the internet unconsciously, you may get benefits from it. You may also get lost in different sites, which may cause you harm. One of my friends told me a funny story. One day, he was watching bowling videos of a Pakistani cricketer on YouTube, who is famous for his speed and taking wickets. He was keenly watching his best wicket videos and noticed another about a scandal related to the cricketer, so he clicked on it. As he opened it, other related videos opened up, too. He started watching those and after some time, he found himself watching porn. My friend taught me an exceptional lesson in a hilarious way—the internet (a tool) unconsciously misled him. This can affect us too, and we can end up harming instead of building ourselves. Our mind is like a super computer. If we use it unconsciously and are not aware of what we are doing, it can harm us, so to take full benefits from it, we have to use it consciously.

To use our mind properly and gain benefits from it, we should understand how it works and what its mechanics are. The best analogy to understand the mind is to compare it to a computer. Computers have an operating system, which is called windows. Humans also have a very advanced window or operating system, which is the mind. Computers have by-default apps, and other apps can be installed into it. Similarly, our mind has also some default apps, and some can be installed into it. If we identify what our default apps are and how we can install others, we can maximize the benefits from it.

Let's talk about a few by-default apps of the human mind. For instance, we have a beautiful app called love. The purpose of love is to develop a long-term relationship and to make a family. The purpose of parental love is to bring up their children in a stable and happy home. That's why every parent loves their children because of parental love app activation. Another by-default app is lust. The purpose of lust is to reproduce, so the Creator put pleasure into the mix to motivate humans to fulfil this purpose. The primary purpose of lust is to reproduce, and the secondary purpose is pleasure. However, most humans are unaware of the primary and secondary purposes. They prioritize the second purpose and, in most cases, with multiple partners leading to the contraction of diseases (STD) and psychosocial problems. Hunger is another app which motivates us to eat food. When we eat food, it gives us satisfaction, so this app was designed by the Creator through which humans can energize themselves. If there was no hunger and no pleasure in it, lots of humans would stop eating because they don't know the true value of life. They just follow pleasure. The primary purpose of eating food is to energize our body and stay alive, and the secondary purpose is pleasure. Some people just do it for pleasure and make themselves unhealthy. One of my friends believes the bravest person in this world is the one who can eat more. These people live for food, but we should eat food to live, not the other way around. If someone is aware of their hunger app and its primary purpose, they can easily maintain their body weight and prevent many diseases.

When these apps are activated, they hijack our conscious mind, and we get lost in it. If a person falls in love, this means their love app is activated, and they are not aware of it, which means love takes over the conscious mind. The infatuation stage of love can be beautiful but also toxic. Many suicides and murder cases have occurred when the consciousness was hijacked by love. This is the same problem with lust. When it is activated, it overcomes an individual's consciousness, which then leads to situations such as rape, child abuse, having multiple partners, and seeking out prostitutes. This can have negative effects on one's health. These apps overcome the human mind when there is little to no awareness of our consciousness. If we are aware of our body, mind, emotions, and thoughts, we can choose to use them to our benefit or for their primary purposes.

We can download new apps into our operating system (mind), like reading, writing, self-defense, cooking, mindfulness, driving, productivity tactics, and more. We can also strengthen or update other apps like emotional intelligence, discipline, concentration, awareness, communication, and many more. How can we install or update these apps into our mind? By rewiring our subconscious mind. We can do this by repeatedly practicing a specific activity. For instance, if you want to learn how to drive, you have to practice. If you want to improve your concentration levels, practice different meditation techniques. Our conscious mind can help us to rewire our subconscious mind. What we do in the present moment is imprinted in our subconscious, so we can choose the activity consciously and purposefully and do that activity repeatedly. A beautiful quote by Kevin Michel states, "To shift your life in a desired direction, you must powerfully shift your subconscious."

In brief, if we know and understand the mechanics of our mind, use it consciously, and rewire our subconscious as we want it, we can easily become more successful and happier.

Chapter 22

CLEAN YOUR MIND ON A REGULAR BASIS.

When we clean our room and get things organized, it becomes dirty and disorganized again after a few days. Is it possible to clean our room once, and it remains clean and organized forever? No, our room becomes dirty because we use it. If we use an analogy that our mind is like our room and we use our mind more than our rooms, what will happen if we don't clean it regularly? Will it remain organized and clear? Do we clean our minds? If yes, how often? Here, I'll use the room analogy to discuss how our minds become dirty and how we can prevent it. If we clean our room on a regular basis, we will always keep it clean and organized. To do this, we need to identify those habits which make our room dirty, i.e., entering a room with dirty shoes or keeping your windows open all the time. We need to identify these issues so that we can avoid them. The same kind of intervention is needed to keep our minds clean. Identification and prevention of bad habits is the first step, and in case we make our mind dirty, we should clean it regularly. So, what makes our mind dirty? Everything that is negative, immoral, and illegal. You know exactly what I am talking about.

Dirty minds don't see things clearly and usually get lost in negative thoughts and activities, which produce negative emotions, such as jealousy, stress, hate, aggression, irritation, depression, and addiction. The less you care about it, the dirtier it becomes. You should frequently ask yourself these two questions. What makes my mind dirty, and how should I keep my mind clean and clear? Different methods have been used by every religion to keep the mind clean and clear, i.e., Muslims pray five times a day, Christians attend church on Sunday, and Buddhists meditate every day. Religion has prohibited certain activities, i.e., consuming alcohol, drugs, backbiting, jealousy, and lying to name a few, which can cause our mind to be dirty. You should follow these rules, and additionally, you can make your own plans and strategies for keeping your mind clear.

The best strategy is to act immediately if you find yourself in an activity which is negative, immoral, and illegal and can make your mind dirty and foggy. For example, if you show aggression to someone or hurt someone and you realize you are doing so, stop and apologize. If you realize it later, make sure you apologize. You can also adopt some exercises on a regular basis to keep your mind clean and clear, like yoga, meditation, prayer, and other positive things. Don't let your mind get dirty and clear it up on a regular basis, which will make your life more creative and blissful. Avoid negative activities which have the potential to harm your mind, body, and relationships, and partake in positive activities. Doing this can heal us, make us smarter and healthier, strengthen our relationships with our loved ones, and spread love to the whole world.

Chapter 23

AVOID FORBIDDEN ACTIVITIES.

You may have heard the story of Adam and Eve and the forbidden fruit. Adam and Eve were ordered not to eat a specific fruit, but they could eat anything else. They were enjoying paradise until Satan misled them, resulting in them eating the forbidden fruit. After eating it, they were expelled from paradise and suffered a lot afterwards but were forgiven later after seeking forgiveness from Allah. There are many deep meanings and lessons in this story, and many great scholars have interpreted these lessons. They interpreted that the forbidden fruit was the tree of knowledge, which revealed the difference between good and evil, and the serpent symbolized evil power. If you are interested in deeper lessons, you should read other scholars' interpretations. I am not a scholar. I am just an ordinary man, and my ordinary mind infers one direct message from this story. Please do not quote me on this because it is just a positive random thought from my mind. If you are able to connect with my interpretation, then that's a positive outcome.

For me, the fruit symbolizes desire because we humans have a natural desire for fruits. After all, eating them gives us some satisfaction. Satan, or a serpent, symbolizes evil, which does not reside in us, but it comes from external sources. That means there are two powers which can attract us to the forbidden fruit: our own desire and evil power from outside of us. We should control both to avoid the forbidden fruit. The simple and direct message in this story is to stay away from prohibited things, whether the desire comes from inside or outer evil forces are manipulating you. Otherwise, it will have adverse outcomes and drag you to failure. These thoughts were activated in my mind after reading a story in a newspaper about a girl who had been sexually assaulted by her own father for one year. He had filmed her naked body and repeatedly raped her. The police found the videos, and the man was arrested and jailed for 10 years. This is an extreme case of human mind dysfunctionality and what happens when we get lost in our forbidden desires. This evil man destroyed his life and that of his family. This man was 60 years old, and after 10 years, he will be 70. At this age, people contract different diseases, i.e., diabetes, hypertension, and heart attacks. He may die in jail, or if he survives, completes his sentence, and gets out of jail, who will accept him back into society? Nobody. He will have no one to take care of him during these crucial years and have only himself to blame. So, one forbidden habit, or in other words, eating one forbidden fruit, destroyed his life and put him in the worst level for failure.

Another big story from Hollywood is the one about Harvey Weinstein, a well-known American film producer who was sentenced to 23 years in jail for rape and sexual assault. He went to jail one day before his 68th birthday. He could have avoided this by controlling his own desires and being aware of being manipulated by others. Simply put, his own desires and external evil trapped him. The news is full of these stories, meaning that many people are falling into the forbidden fruit trap. Everyone has a chance or probability of falling into different kinds of traps. If we want to save ourselves, we have to avoid the forbidden activities and remain aware of our desires and evil around us. Extreme cases begin from pursuing simple forbidden desires, a smoker who starts smoking occasionally and with the passage of time becomes a chain smoker. They are also prone to consuming marijuana and other hard drugs, too. The point I'm trying to make is every prohibited activity begins as every day unconscious habits, i.e., drinking alcohol or watching porn occasionally can lead to addictions and in extreme cases, acts such as rapes and murder, which destroys lives. So, we have to avoid any forbidden activity even if it seems small to us.

In brief, we should avoid any prohibited activities, whether small or big, and train ourselves to perform activities, which will help us grow and have a positive impact on our lives and others. We can avoid these forbidden activities when we are aware of our desires and the evil around us.

Chapter 24

ABOUT AWARENESS.

Which part of us has the potential to control things and retain autonomy? I had searched for the answer to this question for a long time until I realized that it is awareness. This thought sprang to me – "I am not the mind; I am not the body; I am the awareness." The mind and the body are our tools, the best tools we are blessed with. They are not simple tools but sophisticated and intelligent and have infinite value. In those moments when we have no awareness, our complex and highly intelligent tools can take control of us and accomplish desires, convinced by information received from the environment and life experiences. Our bodies may take control and do what it's designed and coded for, even if these actions are immoral and illegal. The body has the coding present in our chromosomes received from parents as well as molded by our psychosocial experiences. We are not born with these factors but acquire our genetic disposition and mindset. They are necessary for us to function in this world under the supervision of awareness.

To identify ourselves as either body or mind is not wise because if someone identifies himself as the body, the body changes with time. From childhood to adulthood, our bodies change, and we look different. That's why people, especially actresses and actors, become depressed when they get older: they identify themselves as only a body and then the youthful looks fade away with time. If someone loses their body parts because of an accident or disease, they become depressed. In society, we treat the differently abled individuals in such a negative way that those who can't use their limbs anymore fall into a depressive state because they have identified themselves as just a body. If someone identifies themselves as mind, the mind also changes with time. The mind can be an unreliable tool, depending on our level of awareness. Sometimes when we are not in a healthy mental state, our mind can exacerbate the situation because we have conditioned it in that way. One can easily forget some essential details. The older you get, the higher chances your memory may start to fade away. Think about diseases, such as dementia and amnesia, and how they affect the mind. If someone identifies themselves as an awareness or presence, they remain constant with the passage of time and can grow by performing spiritual exercises, i.e., prayer or meditation. So, you are not the body or the mind, but you are the awareness.

Those people who commit crimes and wallow in negative activities lack awareness from their mind and body, so that's why they lose control and unconsciously perform whatever their deep unconscious mind commands of them. My favorite positive thought is if a person is not aware of their thoughts, how can they control or change it? For example, if someone's lust app is activated and they are not aware of it, they will perform activities the lust app demands. Or if someone's revenge app is activated, they will follow their ego blindly without considering future consequences. Awareness is the only faculty which one can use to control thoughts and emotions. Once we regain control, we are able to use our mind and body for the activities which have positive outcomes in our lives. Now the important question is, how we can increase our awareness because the more we are aware, the more we have control of ourselves. We should search and adopt practices and techniques which can improve our awareness and control of our lives.

In conclusion, to regain control of our lives, we have to control our mind and body through developing our awareness. If you are wondering what we should do to improve awareness, you should begin by increasing your knowledge bank. Start reading books by spiritual teachers and learn things from them. You must practice what you learn. There are different practices and techniques you can use and you can perform these practices solo or together, i.e., some days you should practice mindfulness, other days you can focus on breathing techniques, or you can do these practices in combination, like writing and yoga.

Chapter 25

PEOPLE'S PERCEPTIONS.

How a person perceives things depends on several factors, such as their knowledge, background, interests, and intelligence. For instance, imagine a beautiful, huge, green tree, then imagine a man looking at it, who is also a botanist. How will he perceive the tree? He is a botanist and has more knowledge about trees than an ordinary man, so he might perceive that tree as a living being and think about how the leaves photosynthesize and how the xylem and phloem transfer water and minerals from the roots to the branches and the importance of this to our ecosystem. Now, imagine a carpenter who is looking at this huge beautiful green tree. How will he perceive this tree? He might think this tree is valuable if he cuts it down and makes some beautiful furniture from it. He sees it as a resource, not a living being. Now, imagine a young boy who can see the beautiful birds set on the branches of the tree. A boy is interested in this tree because of the birds he wants to hunt down with his air gun. Imagine an anxious and depressed person, who is sitting close to the tree but doesn't notice the tree and its beauty because he is wallowing in his anxious and depressing thoughts. Now, think of a spiritual person near the tree. He will perceive this tree as a great wonder and might think how it contributes to the life cycle and makes the world more beautiful. He will see the tree as a beautiful creature from the Creator and think about how intelligently the Creator designed it. The point I want to make here is that there is only one tree, but different people will perceive the tree and its value differently.

Similarly, we are perceived by other people according to their background, knowledge, and state of mind (negativity or positivity). Different people perceive us differently. Some perceive us as beautiful or intelligent, and others perceive us as stupid or ugly. You should not mind if someone makes some snide comments because it's their own perception, and you have nothing to do with their perceptions or opinions. If their perception is negative, they must be a narrow-minded person. They are reflecting on what is within them. They might be living in an illusion because those who are connected with reality see humans as super intelligent and beautiful or handsome as well. It does not mean that you look like beautiful stars, like Angelina Jolie or Brad Pitt, but it means the way you are designed—from atom to cell and cells to whole body, mind and presence—is super intelligent and beautiful. People who are negative or live in this illusion always focus on what they are lacking in their lives, which makes them miserable, and when their illusion breaks, they will find themselves in pain so do not mind them. There must be another person who perceives you as valuable, handsome or beautiful, and intelligent. Humans are the best creatures of the universe. We are extremely intelligent and good-looking. If someone is so blinded by their negativity that they miss out on such beauty and intelligence, then there's a problem with their perception, not with your looks or intelligence.

The good news is that we can manage people's perceptions. One of my nursing managers taught me how we can manage people's perceptions when dealing with the care of patients. For your understanding, I will create an imaginary scenario. A nurse or doctor may give their best care and effort to a patient, but the patient dies because of underlying medical conditions. The patient may flatline, and the team leader stops CPR. After announcing the time of death, the team visibly relaxes. One of the doctor's smiles in response to a colleague's remark unrelated to the patient. Through a window, an attendant witness this interaction. Let's suppose they've been standing at the window from the time the patient started to crash (Their heartbeat was decreasing.). The attendant does not understand what is going on, and they can perceive that these doctors are not serious about this patient who died because of the doctors. This can cause a lot of problems because the attendant doesn't have all the information to see the bigger picture. On the other hand, let's suppose a new doctor or nurse is not proficient in their job. They administer the wrong medicine or wrong dose, and the patient dies because of this. They look serious and professional and proceed to posthumously care for the patient. An attendant in the same situation would acknowledge this behavior as appropriate. The point I'm trying to make is that people perceive issues superficially without all the facts. We have touched on how reactive we can be and how humans can jump to conclusions without a second thought to an alternative explanation.

The point my manager was trying to make was that we are observed and perceived 24/7, so we should do our best and take extra care of patients—being kind, communicating in a positive tone, taking the time to listen, sharing smiles—not just so that we can look like we are doing a good job, but also aid in their recovery. This was an essential concept for me that I was really unaware of which means we can manage people's perceptions, too. It works in most job situations. If your boss gives you a task and you accept it with a smile and complete it on time, your boss will perceive you as an efficient employee, and your chances of getting a promotion will increase. It also works at your home. If your dad perceives you as lazy and your spouse perceives you don't love them, a little extra effort can change and manage their perceptions.

In sum, different people perceive things differently according to their background and knowledge. To some, you are handsome or beautiful, and to others, you are not. Positive people always focus on the positive aspect of things, and negative people will always focus on what they lack. The good news is that we can change and manage people's perceptions by adding a little extra effort.

Chapter 26

ACTIONS OUTWEIGH LOOKS.

Most humans are concerned about their looks. In my opinion, the most important thing for a human being is what they do (action) because the body and mind are blessed to us. If we look good, the credit goes to the Creator because he made us this way, but we can take credit for things which we did, are doing, or will be done in the future. When things weren't going well for me, I felt as if neither my parents nor my friends loved me. They aren't concerned about my looks or intelligence, but they are concerned about what I am doing in my life. If we want people to like or love us, we must remain positive. The day will come sooner or later when we will enjoy the fruits of our accumulative continuous positive activities. Even Allah does not judge us on our looks or thinking processes but on our deeds. Activity is the only thing that is our creation, not our possession. Our creation is the only possession we own and nobody can take it away from us. The rest of our possessions, i.e., the body, intelligence, ability to learn are actually not our possessions but those of Allah. We enjoy them because we are blessed with them, and at any time, this can be taken from us. If you want to succeed and pursue a life filled with happiness, focus on your activities because we can change and control our activities, but we cannot change much about our body or looks. Positive activity is the only way to impact our lives, so stop thinking negatively and complaining about how you look and what you have or don't have. You should think about your actions and choose and perform those actions that can make you successful. Those who are successful receive lots of love and admiration from people, no matter how they look.

Chapter 27

EXERCISE

The World Health Organization defines health as, "A state of complete physical, mental, and social well-being and not merely the absence of disease or infirmity." Exercises make us truly healthy because it improves us physically, mentally and socially. We must include exercise in our daily routine and join the gym. If you cannot go to the gym for any reason or do not like workouts, you should choose other activities that you like. Sports such as swimming, basketball, soccer, cricket, and dance, can be used as enjoyable activities. Learning martial arts or joining a martial art academy is also a good choice because you can burn your calories and learn self-defense techniques, ready for use any time to save yourself in life-threatening situations or to confront bullies with confidence.

Exercise makes the muscles strong and provides stability for daily activities. A healthy and robust body also possesses a strong and confident mind, which improves self-esteem, confidence, self-belief, and attraction to the opposite sex. Your relationship with your partner will improve, or if you looking for a relationship, the confidence, self-esteem, and better body shape will attract the opposite sex. Exercise also improves mood and reduces anxiety and depression because of the release of endorphins, which are a hormone and gives us a high. That's why we feel good after a workout. I highly recommend a workout for those who have recently been dumped or have broken up with someone. After the workout, they will feel the same high. Exercise is a better option than pursuing one-sided love because exercise is in your control, and you can do it whenever you want. Said differently, the key to happiness is in your own pocket but in love needs a partner. Here, a useful quote comes to mind, "Never put the key to your happiness in somebody else's pocket."

Exercise also improves sleep patterns and improves memorization and stamina. If you are a student or employee, everyone needs more stamina to increase productivity and remain fresh all day. During exercise, high density lipoprotein, or HDL, is released, which helps our cardiovascular system by removing plaque in our blood vessels. That's why doing regular exercise reduces the risk of cardiovascular disease when you get older. The bottom line is exercising affects every aspect of our lives in a positive way.

Chapter 28

HOW TO USE ISOLATION WISELY?

Some people are sad because they have no friends, and most of the time, they feel alone. For me, they are luckier than those who always have someone around them because people can turn their lonely hours into productive hours, and nobody will distract them. I have made a lot of friends in school, college, and university, but a time comes when those individuals are no longer your best friends. When I was depressed, I decided I would utilize my alone time reading books. Making 'friendship' with books is a wise decision because our other friends have the same level of experience, knowledge, and intelligence, and there is little chance to learn things from them. Instead of wasting time with them, start by reading books written by those who have more experience, knowledge, achievements, and higher positions in society. Alternatively, we can listen to audio versions of books. In these books, they've shared their life experiences, learning points, and thought processes. We will definitely learn from them because they have a higher concentration of knowledge than us. Just like gases spread through diffusion from higher concentration to lower concentration, similarly, knowledge spreads in the same way. By utilizing your time to learn from other great people, you will improve your knowledge, understanding, and decision-making processes, and you will definitely improve the quality of your life situation and socioeconomic status. So, if you are lonely and nobody is around you, be happy because there is no one to distract you from accomplishing your goals. Books can be your friends. Make friends with people like Brian Tracy, Eckhart Tolle, and many more. Their books are waiting for your attention.

Chapter 29

LOVE BEGETS LOVE.

One day, I was in a restaurant eating lunch with my friends. As time passed, I noticed a guy who brought us some free barbecue and offered it to us with such infectious enthusiasm. He exuded so much love and respect in his eyes that we couldn't say no to him. When he left, my mind started to wonder who this guy was. My mind recalled that a few days ago, he had brought his sick mother to the emergency room, and she had had a heart attack. We took good care of her, and we assured him that she was out of danger. It was our duty to do so, but he felt the care and love and that's why he expressed his care and love to us by offering some free barbecue. In that moment, I developed an insight that care begets care, love begets love, and hate begets hate.

Have you watched the movie, *Eat Pray Love*, based on a book written by Elizabeth Gilbert? In the movie, the main character was struggling after her divorce, so she took a trip around the world. She developed good insights and learned different kinds of meditation from a guru since she wanted to find peace in her life. One day, her guru was teaching her a new meditation, "meditation with a smile." She told the guru that she was already smiling, but the guru responded that she should smile with her entire being—from her face to her liver. Then whenever she met someone, she had a smile on her face. It's a strong meditation technique, but if we add love and care with a smile, it becomes stronger. Whenever we are at home or with colleagues, we should have a big smile on our face and send them love through our heart 'Bluetooth' instead of trying to control them. The love we send to others will attract more love, and more love will increase our energy field and frequency to attract creativity, good relationships, peace of mind, and success.

There are people around us who have unconditional love and care for other people, even for strangers. I remember a nice lady, our nursing manager at the emergency room in MSF (*Médecine Sans Frontières*). She was from South Africa, and her name was Anke Yassel. She was with us at MSF for six months. Before completing her mission, she interviewed all the nursing staff in the emergency room department. She also interviewed me and asked a few questions, ranging from what I like to what my hobbies and challenges are. After the interview, I was confused as to why she was conducting interviews.

When she completed her mission and was about to leave, she gave a blessing letter to every staff member. She wrote good wishes to everyone, according to the information she got in her interviews. For example, I told her that I am interested in writing and working on a book. Like me, she was interested in writing and was currently writing blog posts for the MSF website, so she wrote good wishes for my book. What really impressed me was her effort. There were almost 60 staff in the emergency room department, so to interview them all and then write letters for everyone, she needed a lot of time, energy, and love. She was from South Africa and came to the northern area of Pakistan from where Malala Yousafzai belongs (KPK Province of Pakistan), which means we had no cultural, ethnic, or religious relations, but we had one relation—humanity. When she was leaving, we showed our love and care by buying her gifts. She is the only manager that I still remember to date. I admired and respected her for the impact she had on my life.

So, the moral of the story is simple. Love begets love, and hate begets hate. Those who spread love will also attract love, and those who spread hate and aggression will attract hate and aggression.

Chapter 30

YOU ARE SO LUCKY!

People become depressed because of small issues and life challenges. They take extreme measures, such as committing suicide, and they have no idea how lucky they are. Luck is defined as "success or failure brought on by chance rather than through one's own actions," so we do not get live through our own actions. We get to live through chance. In this chapter, we will calculate the chance of getting life. After doing this, we can say how lucky a person is. We can calculate the chance of getting life by calculating the chance or probability of a sperm and an egg making a zygote. To do this, we need two variables. One is the global total fertility rate, and the other is total sperm count that a healthy male can produce their life. According to livescience.com, "Total fertility rate (TFR)—or often simply 'fertility rate'—measures the average number of children per woman. The global average fertility rate is below 2.5 children per woman today." In simple words, the average children per woman is 2.5, so only 2.5 sperm are successful.

According to livescience.com, "The average male will produce roughly 525 billion sperm cells over a life time." That means 2.5 sperm become successful out of 525 billion sperms and win the biggest lottery ever. The prize is life. Now, we know both total fertility rate and total number of sperm an average male produces in their lifetime, so it's easy to calculate the chance or the probability of a single sperm forming a zygote. The formula to calculate the probability is "the probability of an event = (number of favorable outcomes)/(total number of possible outcomes)." In our scenario, the number of favorable outcomes is 2.5, and the numbers of possible outcomes is 525 billion. After calculating it, we get this number 4.7619048e-12 (4.7619048 times ten to the minus twelve powers), or 0.0000000000047619048. So, there is an extremely small chance for a sperm to be successful and win the lottery of life, but the story doesn't end here. The first five years are also crucial. According to World Health Organization, the global infant mortality rate was 29 per 1000 in 2017, so the annual infant deaths were 4.1 million. The point I want to make is the probability or chance for winning the life lottery is extremely small and almost impossible. Everyone agrees that the value of life is infinite but let's allocate a number to this infinite value. It's easy for the mind to concretize the idea. In Chapter 3, we calculated the value of life as 95 thousand trillion dollars. If someone wins 95 quadrillion dollars in a lottery, their chances were less than 0.0000000000047619048 (4.7619048 times ten to the minus twelve powers).

In simple words, suppose someone gives you a free lottery ticket, and the prize is 95 thousand trillion dollars, and only two people can win the lottery out of 525 billion people. What chance does this winner have? It's a minuscule chance but think about how lucky they are. That means every individual who is alive is already extremely lucky, valuable, and successful. On the other hand, imagine that an individual wins a lottery of 95 thousand trillion dollars, and they are still depressed and waste all that money on irrelevant things? What would you think of that person? Are they smart? Are they foolish? By wallowing in negativity, that individual will lose the happiness they deserve. They will waste the money and then complain later. You can only think of them as insane people. The humans who have committed suicide have no idea how lucky and valuable they are. When someone realizes how lucky and valuable, they are, they will never think of taking their own lives. In my opinion, the realization of the true value of being alive is enlightenment. Buddha defines enlightenment as the end of suffering.

To conclude, life is extremely precious and valuable, and we are extremely lucky to be alive. We should be grateful to our Creator. We should also take care of ourselves and other humans, too, because they are extremely valuable.

A NOTE
TO THE READER

I'm glad I was able to put down my thoughts in a somewhat coherent manner. This was my poor effort to realize them. My main message is for those who are feeling depressed and suicidal. You are worthy, and we need you here on earth. Your true potential is yet to be realized and you have a lot more to offer. As an emergency nurse, I saw many parents, spouses, and siblings cry, yearning to hold their loved ones once again. This was painful to watch, so my message is simple—think positively, develop positivity. If you think these positive thoughts in this book have some potential to save people from depression and suicide or can bring positive change in their lives, please share it with others and write an honest review online (Amazon, etc.). Be blessed.

ABOUT THE AUTHOR

Minhaj Uddin is a lecturer in a nursing college. He holds a Bachelor of Science in Medicine (Major in Nursing) from Bahria University Islamabad and also completed Masters in Health Economics and Management from Quaid-I-Azam University Islamabad. He worked in one of the best international humanitarian organization (awarded Nobel Peace Prize in 1999) (Médecins Sans Frontières) as a registered nurse in emergency room and dealt with thousands of patients with anxiety, panic attack, depressed and attempted suicide. He has also observed and experienced life and death very closely during dealing with patients like new born babies, that are springing forth new life, as well as terminally old patients doing the opposite.

In his early thirties, he suffered from depression and overcome this depression episodes by developing new insights by reading spiritual books and from life experiences. His favorite author is Eckhart Tolle and his favorite book is The Power of Now.

Minhaj is currently living in Swat valley, the northern area of Pakistan.

www.ingramcontent.com/pod-product-compliance
Lightning Source LLC
Chambersburg PA
CBHW060038040426
42331CB00032B/1016